Praise for *An Honest Day's Work*

"Chris Atkins is one of the very best public relations professionals and a fabulous story teller…perhaps they always were meant to go hand-in-hand. *An Honest Day's Work* is a great read, full of anecdotes that all of us can relate to. Read his book. You will learn a lot and chuckle along the way."

—*Chris Komisarjevsky, retired Global CEO,*
Burson-Marsteller

"Chris Atkins' delightful memoir of his adventures in the spin trade manages to be both very funny and, at the same, affectionate about the rich characters he has met along the way. Anyone who has worked in the field will instantly recognize the delicious tension he describes between the outward face of public events and the private work that makes them happen."

—*Peter Hirsch, Director, Reputation Risk,*
Ogilvy Public Relations

"From publicity stunts to crisis management, Chris shares experiences that span four decades with wit, insight and not a little irony. Chris leads us through the labyrinth of a public relations man's not-so-sentimental education. It's an engaging journey."

—*Irv Schenkler, Associate Professor, Stern School of Management,*
New York University

"I've had the unique privilege to work alongside Chris Atkins and also call him a friend. As a PR veteran myself, I can tell you *An Honest Day's Work* is one of the most engrossing, educational and laugh-out-loud funny explorations of life in the wonderful world of PR I've read. It's a must read for anyone in—or aspiring to be in—our crazy profession."

—*Steve Cody, cofounder and CEO, Peppercomm*

catkins702@gmail.com
laurenletellier@gmail.com

An
Honest
Day's Work

To Joe Fusco
Who Always Puts In
An Honest Day's Work!

C Atkin

Chris Atkins

An Honest Day's Work

True Tales of a Life in PR

Pill Hill Productions

Published by Pill Hill Productions
P.O. Box 706, Hillsdale, NY 12529

This book is a memoir and is drawn from my own experience. For the most part, I have used real names, but if I felt that a story or reference might be embarrassing or unpleasant, I dropped last names or used pseudonyms.

Cover design by Alex Head/Draft Lab

Cover image © iStock.com/Chic Type

ISBN 13: 978-0-9907815-1-6

Contents

Preface

FOR YEARS, I HAVE HAD the pleasure of amusing colleagues and friends with stories about my career in public relations. Almost always, someone encourages me to write a book about these experiences. About 15 years ago, I decided to give it a try but found that I lacked the motivation and attention span to get more than a few pages done and then the pressures of work conspired against me. I also had to consider the impact that publishing a memoir might have on my future employment prospects.

Now, as my corporate career gives way to the luxury of consulting, writing and teaching for a living, I have the time. While I am less concerned about offending potential employers or clients, I've nevertheless resisted the urge to write a tell-all gossip fest. I have found such works by other authors to be boring, bitter and unsatisfying to read.

What I have focused on are anecdotes that bring to life why it is almost impossible to be bored in PR. Something wonderful or ridiculous is always just around the corner, and while I may have been a little stressed by these events at the time, looking back they add up to a career I would not have traded for any other.

I ran parts of the manuscript by a few people whose opinion I greatly respect, and one of them made an interesting point. "You seem to focus more on the screw-ups than on the many successes in which you were involved. Admittedly, some of the screw-ups turned out positively."

He's right. But I can't imagine anything as inauthentic (and yawn-inducing) than a series of "wonderful me" anecdotes, and I think the failures or "saves" are way more revealing. That's why I am always underwhelmed by agency case studies, which frequently have a *Deus Ex Machina* quality about them.

A word about the title: Anyone in the PR business is aware of the negative image we have in the minds of some—not all—reporters. They profess to see us as professional obfuscators, barriers to their pursuit of the Fourth Estate's sacred mission: ensuring the public's right to know. (Some are less strident and appreciate the access they get to senior leaders, which would never happen without the aid of the PR person.)

In 35 years as a practitioner, not one client or employer has ever come close to asking me to misrepresent the truth. I have made the decision from time to time, given the angle of a reporter's story and his or her prior reporting, not to allow access to the boss, which inevitably leads the reporter to suspect that we had something to hide. I think it's telling that there has been a lot more news in the last decade about reporters inventing stories and plagiarizing content than about PR people being less than truthful.

Yet the canard that PR people are "spinmeisters," "shills," and "reckless liars" persists, in bars where reporters hang out and sometimes in their reporting. Gil Schwartz, longtime head of PR for CBS Corporation, became something of a folk hero in the PR world when he appeared on CBS *Sunday Morning* to chastise a jerky *Sunday Morning* commentator who had recently set his sights on the PR profession. It makes for amusing viewing—you can look it up on YouTube.

So the stories in this book are *real* accounts of events in my career, which I hope I have recounted in a way that minimizes embarrassment for anyone but in all other ways are exactly as I remember them.

I hope you enjoy it. It has been a great ride for me.

—C.A.

Chapter One

Canoes and Commas

IN 1980, MY FRIEND ERIC King was working as the assistant sales manager for Grumman Boats. They were part of the same Grumman that built many of the fighter planes used in WWII and whose lunar module put Neil Armstrong on the moon. This division made boats and canoes. The canoes, in particular, were especially popular with summer camp owners because they were virtually indestructible. Millions of campers had fond memories of paddling around in one.

That's why Grumman kept making them long after it was profitable to maintain such a tiny division: Roy Grumman always believed that the memories of summer fun at camp warmed the hearts of the congressmen and Pentagon staffers to whom the company was so beholden. (I have been told that it's the same reason Johnson & Johnson still makes baby products, even though they bring in a tiny percentage of J&J's profits. The emotional connection for most people is transcendent.)

Grumman Boats had for years retained a one-man PR shop in Manhattan—Rockwell & Newell. Dwight Rockwell started the business in 1975 with book publicist Ellie Newell. By the time I got there, he was in his mid-50s. Newell had moved on a long time before, but Dwight liked the symmetry of Rockwell & Newell. Plus, he'd once ordered 144 ballpoint pens embossed with the name from an in-flight magazine, and nothing was going to change until the supply of pens dried up.

Dwight was a great guy but a bit of a one-trick pony. His specialty was getting the senior editor of Outdoor Life magazine to run quarterly special features on camping and fishing expeditions, which always prominently featured a Grumman canoe. He usually undertook these adventures by meeting the editor in one of the backwoods watering holes that punctuated the side streets east and west of Madison Avenue. They served Bombay martinis deep enough to sink in up to your elbow when fishing out the lemon twist, which Dwight liked to nibble on. At this, Dwight was a master.

But Dwight had one weakness: although he was suave and self-assured, he could not have written a grammatically correct gravestone. And he was overly fond of exclamation points. If he *had* ever written a grave marker, it would probably have read:

Here Lies Joe Blow!
Born 1905, Died 1977!!!

He also had a tendency to use such literary pearls as, "Also and in addition…" The Grumman folks were constantly grousing about the atrociously written press release drafts they received from Dwight and they finally issued an ultimatum. "Either hire someone who can write or we're taking our business elsewhere."

Eric King suggested that Dwight meet with me, because I was a good writer, unemployed and cheap. This was all music to Dwight's ears. I went down to Manhattan to meet with him, and after about 90 minutes of conversation, he offered me a job as a writer for $200 a week. I did the arithmetic and decided I could make that work, although it would not have been feasible if he hadn't paid me in cash. Paying taxes would have ruined the economics. (A couple of years later, the IRS sent me a letter that ruined my day—I hadn't realized that Dwight was deducting my salary on his taxes as a business expense.)

It was $25 more than I was making as a substitute teacher. Despite the fact that I had an education degree, I really had no interest in teaching. I had wanted to become a journalist, in fact.

I started my college education at George Washington University (GW) in the fall of 1973 because their J-School was (and still is) highly regarded. Washington, D.C., like the rest of the country, had just become captivated by the Watergate scandal, and my classmates and I dreamed of being Carl Bernstein or Bob Woodward. But instead of studying the secrets of digging up the big scoop, I found myself wallowing morosely in the History of Journalism 101. The typical impatience of a freshman with an unrequited passion took hold of me and in just one semester I concluded that I had made a big mistake.

I spent a few semesters trying other majors, landed on psychology for a bit, and then took stock of my growing debt and stultifying coursework and decided to take a break. I took a job in D.C. as a driver for the now defunct Emery Air Freight, which was ironic given the many years I spent leading the FedEx account team at PR firm Ketchum years later. Eventually I had to admit to myself that my "10-4-Good-Buddy" CB radio life did not comport with my self-image and headed back to school at State University of New York College at Cortland. I cross-referenced my GW transcript with the Cortland degree requirements to see which major, after transferring my GW credits, would allow me to graduate in the shortest amount of time: Voila! Education. After school, I moved up to Lake Placid with a friend, got a job bussing tables and applied for a job with the Olympic Committee (the winter games in 1980 were held in Lake Placid).

A retired army master sergeant was in charge of transportation, and the Emery Air Freight experience caught his eye, especially the fact that I had filled in as a dispatcher from time to time. He offered me the job of senior dispatcher for the Official Transportation department. Four bucks an hour, plus overtime and a free pass to all Olympic events. Of course, I worked 18-hour days for the entire two weeks and only managed to see the last half of the closing ceremonies.

With no job prospects in sight, I spent the spring substitute teaching. When I met Dwight I was tutoring a couple of ninth graders who could not be bothered to walk an extra five feet off school property to smoke a joint during a school dance. They were suspended for the rest of the term, but state law required that they be taught anyway. It was the only teaching experience I ever had, and it was like teaching remedial earth science to Cheech and Chong.

So you could say I was looking for something to do with my life. Of course, when I showed up for my first PR job on June 16, 1980, I didn't really know what PR was.

#

I worked for Dwight Rockwell for two years. It was mostly fun, and I was writing copy every day and talking to reporters, honing my fledgling PR skills. Every now and then, Dwight would take me along on one of his media placement benders, and afterwards we would go back to the office and sit, semi-paralyzed, for the rest of the afternoon. A person walking through the door would have thought he had encountered two stroke victims for all the coherence we could muster. Eventually, we would part for the evening, to Beekman Place for him, Brooklyn for me. I would have my customary dinner—a bag of corn chips and a Heineken for a buck and a half at the corner bodega.

Oddly enough, like an art critic who has never painted anything other than his living room, Dwight had some rather strong opinions about writing, which he dispensed liberally and with a bit of misplaced exasperation. "How many times do I have to tell you, verbs are the bullets in the writer's gun." He had a point. Why "attract" media attention when we can "seize" it? Exciting verbs demonstrate passion and enthusiasm for a new initiative, and give a piece of copy a sense of urgency and action.

More wisdom from Dwight: "Six words are better than seven—way better than ten." Trust me, less really is more. I can remember Dwight not only counting words but also the number of letters in certain words in order to say the most with the least. Okay, he did have many of the telltale signs of clinical depression. Nonetheless it was a lesson that stayed with me over the years. Daniel Webster said that the better he got at writing, the more "scratch outs" he did. This is much easier to do today than it was when I first started, since way back then a significant copy change meant ripping the sheet from the typewriter and starting all over again.

I had my first and only brush with advertising in that job. Dwight was out of town and I got a call from Grumman saying that they were exhibiting in a boat show and were buying an ad in the show magazine. They needed something fast, so I set to work. I decided to find just the right graphic and then come up with a catchy headline. We had files and files of photography. Dwight was always sending out freelance photographers to capture images of Grumman products *in situ* and in no time I found the shot I wanted.

It was an action shot of a young man driving a Grumman speedboat. The guy was wearing only swimming trunks, and when I say that he was the archetype for the 98-pound weakling, I am being too kind. But his passenger, on the other hand, was a dead ringer for Pamela Sue Anderson, resplendent in a bikini. How they got these two in the same boat is a mystery, but there it was. At the speed they were going, he should have been focused on the water ahead, but not surprisingly, his eyes were glued on her. His tongue wasn't quite hanging out, but it was close.

My headline: "Parts of your life have no room for compromise. Your boat is one of them." A little cheesy, but at least it might shore up the client's 98-pound weakling sales deficit. The client loved the ad, and sent it off to the Grumman corporate legal department. The lawyer who reviewed the ad was skeptical and called his boss, who was on a business trip. The lawyer described the ad over the phone as semi-pornographic (it certainly was not!) and not in keeping with Grumman's military-style culture (possibly true). Without ever seeing it, the boss demanded that the girl in the picture be airbrushed out.

Thus ran what may have been the dumbest ad in history: a photo of a skinny, goofy-looking nerd in a boat leering lustfully at the vacant seat next to him with a headline that absolutely defied any comprehension.

I told Dwight about it upon his return. He laughed so hard I thought he might cough up a lemon twist. But clearly, this PR guy's advertising career was over.

#

Part of my job was to respond when reporters called looking for information. Usually, they wanted the basic specifications of a boat or canoe; sometimes they wanted a picture. But one frigid day in January, I got a call from a writer with a national publication asking what seemed a simple enough question: "How many people go canoeing each year in the United States?" And this turned out to be a great lesson in the illusory nature of statistics.

I didn't have any idea how many people canoed each year, but I promised to get back to him as soon as I could. When I hung up the phone, I asked Dwight if he had any idea. He was just back from a three-martini safari with a journo on 47th Street, and was his usual helpful post-luncheon self.

"What kind of a dumb-ass question is that? How the hell should I know? Go find out!"

I started by asking the client.

"Geez, nobody has ever asked that before." Sigh. So we began looking at the number of canoes Grumman sold each year, and then estimated the sales of the other major brands on the market. Then we called a few Grumman dealers who maintained canoe rental operations and got some help there. The National Marine Manufacturers Association dug up some not-too-old market data and we added that to the mix. Then we looked at the circulation figures for magazines like *Outdoor Life* and *Sports Afield*, on the theory that some percentage of their readers would occasionally paddle a canoe.

By day's end we had assembled quite a collection of data, none of which answered the question but taken in total provided a foundation of wet sand upon which to build a Wild Ass Guess: Six million Americans went canoeing each year.

I called the reporter and gave him the answer. He thanked me and hung up. I didn't think about it again until spring, when the magazine ran a piece on outdoorsy things to do with one's family, and lo! There it was: "According to the folks at Grumman Canoes, six million Americans take a canoe trip each year."

Nice hit. The client was happy. Dwight yawned and looked at his watch—almost time for a lunch-time bivouac with an editor from Times Mirror.

About five years later, I was flipping through an in-flight magazine and came upon an article about camping and canoeing opportunities. And there it was again: "According to industry sources, six million Americans take a canoe trip each year." It didn't mention

Grumman but by then I had moved on to another agency and they were not my clients anymore. I was just intrigued by the durability of a number that had all the soundness of a White House jobs report—well, okay, maybe my number had a little more statistical validity than that.

In the late '90s, I happened on an article about water-based recreation that cited this statistic: "Some seven million Americans canoe each year." Curious, I called the writer, who told me the source was the PR firm for a canoe manufacturer (not Grumman). It must have been a slow day because I went to the trouble of digging up the number of the Midwestern PR firm and in due course got to the right person. I asked where the number seven million came from, and he admitted (as a professional courtesy, I guess) that he and his client came up with it by adding one million to the six million they'd found cited in the 1980s. The extra million was to account for the passage of time! It seemed just as reasonable as my approach.

Whenever I hear someone cite a statistic of one kind or another, I think of my experience and I wonder if anybody's numbers are any more valid than the one I cooked up.

#

Dwight was a classy guy who could also act with a stunning lack of grace when he was in one of his frequent depressions, usually brought on by an argument with his much-younger girlfriend. When my first marriage was impending, I of course sent Dwight an invitation to the wedding. When he came in to the office a couple of days later, he tossed the invitation on my desk. "Decline with regrets. Add a nice note." He was serious! For the benefit of my future mother-in-law, I wrote a very gracious and flattering note extolling my virtues as an employee. I signed his name and stuck it in the mail. (M-I-L: "And your boss said such *nice things* about you!")

Before I convinced Dwight to invest in a postage meter, he would dispatch me to the post office to buy sheets of perforated stamps. After one such trip, I returned with an envelope of perfectly good United States first-class postage. Dwight took one look and said, "What the fuck is this?"

"What the fuck is what?" I replied, a little preoccupied with loading a new ribbon into my typewriter.

"This!" he said, waving a sheet of stamps under my nose. "These are *Martin Luther King* stamps. Don't you realize we send our press releases to writers all over the south? They'll just throw them away without opening them. Take these back and get something else."

I tried, but the post office did not accept returns. So until we used them up, I had to make sure that we only put them on envelopes addressed to places well above the Mason-Dixon line.

And cheap? Dwight was apoplectic when the New York Taxi and Limousine Commission mandated a rush-hour surcharge of fifty cents. I can't remember why, but at first, the surcharge was approved for independent cab owners, but not fleet owners. Or maybe it was the other way around. In any case, for a short period of time, you could not be sure if the cab was going to ding you for the half-a-buck surcharge until you got in. Dwight was incensed!

Eventually I finally found another job. At the end of my last day, we left the office together. The last time I saw Dwight, he was hailing a cab on Madison. He opened the back door and yelled, "Do you charge the extra fifty cents? Yes? Well move along then, I don't want to ride in your goddamn cab." On the third try, he got in and the cab took off, those two quarters safe in Dwight's fraying Brooks Brothers suit pocket.

Interlude:
Debate Punctuation on Facebook?
You'd Be an Asterisk It.

If you want to provoke a raging argument on Facebook, forget about politics or religion. Try asking a question about punctuation.

A while back, I started a blog called "Chris Atkins' Random PR Thoughts." Almost immediately, I was castigated by an extraordinarily literate Facebook friend for the punctuation of the name of my blog. She contended that the possessive form of my last name should be "Atkins's." I was taught in seventh grade that to make a name that ends with an "s" possessive, one simply adds an apostrophe. No extra "s" is required.

I checked a couple of style manuals and learned that there is no consensus on this point. The AP and Chicago style manuals say no extra "s", while the renowned Strunk & White insists on it. I put out a call on FB, and I might as well have added, "Let slip the dogs of war!"

Perhaps because so many of my FB friends are accomplished writers, punctuation tends to be a bit of an emotional issue. Ask, "Does the period go inside or outside the parentheses?" Then pour yourself a glass of wine and get ready to rumble.

If you dare, ask about the Oxford comma. That's the comma that some say should follow each item in a list of three or more items, as in "Apples, oranges, and pears." Some style manuals dictate that the last comma should be deleted: "Apples, oranges and pears." I first learned to use the Oxford comma, and then was forced in school to eliminate it. It was rather like the way, in the early years of the last century, lefties were forced to learn to write with their right hands. Losing the Oxford comma was really uncomfortable at first but eventually it became natural to me.

Another reason some people get so worked up about grammar and punctuation may also stem from the unintended (and often hilarious) outcomes from errors in usage. Consider the sentence, "I will help my uncle, Jack, off the horse" without the commas. And that's enough about that!

Chapter Two

Dial-and-Smile!

THE MONDAY AFTER I LEFT Rockwell & Newell, I reported for duty at Geltzer & Co., a 30-person shop run by a husband and wife team, Howard and Sheila Geltzer. Their offices were in a swanky building on Broadway, and Howard and Sheila had a very cool tradition of hosting a brunch for clients and staff on Thanksgiving morning. Our fifth floor offices afforded an outstanding view of the Macy's Thanksgiving parade, whose giant balloons were right at eye level. It was the only time I ever saw the parade live *and* warm.

Apart from that cozy memory, the place was pretty intense. After working for Dwight Rockwell, I recognized the behavior of owners who took home the last check each month. Each of the staff had an antique electric typewriter and no two were alike. Mine was a sleek blue number from Smith Corona. After about nine months, the "e" stopped working. I asked the office manager if I could get it serviced, and she grunted something. Whatever it was, nobody showed up. I had to borrow someone else's machine to get my work done.

Finally, in frustration and anger, I sat down in front of my broken typewriter and pounded out four pages of copy—with a space wherever there was supposed to be an "e." Then I wrote in each missing "e" with a pen and sent my copy on to Sheila for review.

My machine was fixed the next day, but I am betting there was a bit of discussion about the cost/benefit ratio—we did have a lot of Bic pens.

My account was Ingersoll-Rand, which made, among other things, enormous air compressors to power factory equipment. My job was to write stories about these machines, and then place them in the few obscure trade publications whose readers would give a hoot.

A few of us banged out nearly 100 of these case histories in my 18 months of employment, yet to this day I have never actually laid eyes on one of these massive machines. The agency was paid a flat rate per story—the fee covered research, writing and placement. It wasn't enough money to cover travel, so we did all the research and interviews by phone.

> Me: So, I hear you have a new KCB-5000. How's that working out for you?
>
> Plant Manager: Well, we like it fine. It does a real nice job for us.

I had to keep this guy talking until I could tease out four pages of copy—1,000 words!—about a machine that blew air into a hose.

A few words about how air compressors—specifically rotary-screw air compressors—work. They suck air into a chamber that typically has two rotors that look like big screws with threads. These rotors pull the air into the threads and squish it until the air comes whizzing out the other end like a bullet from a gun. As the rotors do their work, they get really hot—so hot that they would burn up if they were not fed a constant stream of lubricant.

But Ingersoll-Rand had developed a compressor with a whole new rotor design that compressed the air just as well as the old design but was so precisely engineered it did not need lubrication.

One day, the client called and breathlessly announced that they'd just sold a "next generation" air compressor. This was huge! We needed to get this in *Compressed Air* magazine as soon as possible.

I got the plant manager on the phone. His company, based in Indianapolis, made snack foods and was appropriately named Snack Foods, Inc.

> Me: So, I hear you got yourself a new CLF-8000. How's that working out for you?
>
> Plant Manager: We like it just fine. It gives us clean, lubricant-free compressed air and we're gonna save a ton on air filters.
>
> Me: How's that?
>
> Manager: Well you don't need filters if the air comes out without lubricant.
>
> Me: Without lubricant, you say. Is that important?
>
> Manager: Is that important? Let me tell you, Sonny, a drop of lubricant on your corn doodle will ruin your whole day!

That quote was the pinnacle of my case history career. Because of it, I was able to place a story about the compressor in *Popular Mechanics*. It was a feat never before achieved by my client and which, I am willing to bet, never happened again. I basked in the glory. The agency gave me a $100 bonus that Christmas—a crappy bonus even back then.

But the discipline, born of sheer desperation, to keep gnawing on a story until it was done was probably the best training I ever had. That job forced me to write every day, and that is the only way you ever get good at it.

One of the agency's accounts was a company that made coupon books for fundraising. The books were published in cities around the country and contained discounts for local establishments. The idea was that you could look through the book and select a restaurant, tear out the coupon and get one free entrée when you ordered another for the same or greater price. Charitable groups would buy the books at wholesale and sell them at retail. The Geltzers gave us each a coupon book for Christmas.

So my bonus was a chance for my wife and I to spend the money to hire a babysitter, travel into the city from the suburbs where we lived, go to a restaurant we'd never tried, and get $9.99 off the bill. Appetizers, drinks and dessert were not included. And you had to present the coupon to the waiter before you ordered, which guaranteed you weren't going to see much of him or her during the meal.

# # #

I had another experience at Geltzer that was formative in a "hope this never happens to you" sort of way. One of Geltzer's clients was Chubb insurance. Among other things, Chubb sold insurance to protect theatrical productions. I was assigned to write a press release about a type of insurance that protected Broadway theaters in case they were unable to go on with the show. My lead was, "Long before the hit show *Dreamgirls* goes on the road, it may find itself on the street, thanks to the demolition of the theater next door." Catchy, huh? I submitted it to my boss and it came back this way: "Long before the hit show *Dreamgirls* goes on the road, it may find itself without a theater ..."

Moral of the story: If you ever find yourself editing someone else's work, try to be a kind editor. Be ruthless about rooting out typos and grammatical errors, but don't edit the fun out of a piece of writing.

#

Chubb had some other interesting product lines that were fun to write about and the stories were easy to place. There was hole-in-one insurance, for example, for country club golf tournaments in which you could win $10,000 for an ace. And a policy that paid $1 million if a lucky fisherman who had paid the $20 fee to enter a fishing contest caught a specially tagged fish that had been released in Lake Michigan—it was a fundraiser for a Chicago charity. The fish lived a long life. (Amazingly, one contestant caught one of the five decoys that also had been released. He won a $5.99 tackle box and a fish story he would tell for the rest of his life.)

One of Chubb's divisions was Surplus Lines, which provided insurance for fine art collections, rare antiques, and even a celebrity athlete's hands. Business was booming and a group of us went out to meet with the division head. This guy was incredibly full of himself, and our day-to-day client was clearly terrified of him. As we entered his large and expensively furnished office, I could see why. I spied a copy of a popular book of the day on his bookshelf. It was called, *Winning Through Intimidation*. But I would have known it was his bible without seeing the book.

He had placed his sofa and armchairs up against the perimeter of the office, with enormous potted shrubs between each seat. There was nowhere to look except at him. His own chair was elevated so that you had to look up to see his face. And throughout our meeting, if one of us started to opine about something, he would pick up his phone and bark something at his long-suffering secretary. "I'm sorry," he would say to whomever was speaking, "Could you repeat that?"

He had an antique clock that would chime like Big Ben every 15 minutes—if at that moment he was talking, he would lower his voice and mumble so we could not hear what he was saying over the bells and to his evident annoyance, we would have to ask him to repeat whatever he had said. That was a long meeting. After precisely one hour, he waved the back of his hand at us to indicate that we were dismissed. As we walked out, our client was trembling and whimpered, "Oh dear, I think you have some fence-mending to do with him." I thought it would be best if we could just brick up his doorway.

The halls of the Geltzer offices were decorated with big foam boards displaying some of the best media hits we had gotten for our clients. It really was a badge of honor to have one of your hits on the wall, and it didn't seem likely that a story about an air compressor was going to get me there. But Chubb had a line of insurance that covered the various mishaps that could befall a movie production company.

The sizzling hot movie at the time was *ET: The Extra Terrestrial* and the media were scrambling to find any little angle that would provide fodder for yet another story about the film. Chubb had insured the production. I went through my dog-eared Bacon's directory of media contacts and dialed Aljean Harmetz, the legendary New York Times Hollywood correspondent. I pitched the Chubb story and to my utter surprise, she bit. In no time, we had her on the phone with the client, and the result was a half-page story about the Chubb product with a big photo of ET.

A couple of weeks later, I came into the office and saw, just next to my door, a foam board with my placement. I could swear that alien winked at me.

Interlude:
Micro Data

You hear the term "Big Data" a lot these days. It seems to be the answer to almost any question that arises:

- How can we predict what our customers will want to buy in six months?
- How can I predict the next financial downturn?
- Where in the US am I most likely to catch the flu?

We're told that the answers to all these questions can be found by analyzing the reams of data now at our disposal. Big Data refers to the collection and analysis of enormous data sets to spot trends and predict outcomes. Some see Big Data and predictive analytics as the next wave of ultra-targeted marketing, while others view this as a dire invasion of privacy. Probably it's a little of both—a candy and a breath mint.

But other than the sheer scale of Big Data, the idea is hardly a new one. The direct mail business has traditionally relied on collecting and analyzing data about potential customers. The theory was that if you had a list of people who had purchased one thing, it would be useful as they were likely to purchase another thing. In Calvin Trillin's amusing novel *Tepper Isn't Going Out*, direct mailer Murray Tepper considers which mailing lists will yield the best sales for a particular product.

The table was, as usual, cluttered with the old-fashioned rate cards that Tepper went through in deciding which lists might be worth testing for whatever was being sold through the mail. Each card described a list that was available for rental—"40,000 buyers of American Revolution decorations and memorabilia" or "61,000 buyers of discount automotive accessories" or "40,000 buyers of deodorizing shoe pads."

Murray was cross-referencing one list with another. You could say that Murray was also engaging in predictive analytics, using the Big Data of his day. If you knew that people on your list who had purchased gambling equipment were twice as likely to purchase electric carving knives, well now—that's data! What else might these dicers and slicers buy? The fun was in the finding out. And it still is, whether you are using a whole server farm or the back of an envelope.

But the most powerful data of all is that which gives you a window into someone's soul. You might call this "micro data."

Like everyone else of my generation, I used to rely on a quaint device known as a Rolodex to organize and store my business contacts. (My personal contacts were in my address book, which was an actual book, not an icon on my desktop.) Early in my career, I knew a guy, a seasoned vet, who used to keep careful notes on the back of each one of his Rolodex cards, along the lines of:

- Jimmy 4-29-79, Susie 6-12-81
- Wife Doris (met @ UMich)
- Larchmont
- Bombay Martini

If the contact was a reporter, there would also be notations about story ideas previously pitched. This was "micro data." If this guy wanted to pitch a story to a reporter, he would be able to start the conversation by asking after spouse and kiddies, getting names and ages right, and suggesting getting together soon for a favorite libation—preferably near Grand Central and the train to Larchmont. And by the way, how about those University of Michigan Wolverines!

It was amazing how well that worked—it turned out that reporters are people too, and just as susceptible to flattery and a kind word as the rest of us. This guy was a media relations machine. Time and again, I saw him make front-page stories appear—or sometimes disappear—through the depth and strength of his relationships.

Chapter Three

Called Up to the Majors

ONE OF THE PEOPLE I met at Geltzer & Co. was a guy named Steve Cody. Steve was much revered by the Geltzers, and his decision to leave the agency was traumatic for them. For the rest of us, it was more than a little inspiring.

I stuffed a copy of my resume in Steve's briefcase just before he left his office for good, bound for Hill and Knowlton. As far as I was concerned, Steve's move was like his being called up to "The Show" from Double-A baseball, and I asked him to keep me in mind once he got settled.

A few weeks later, Steve called me. It turned out that he had been assigned to a new account, Alexander Proudfoot Company, and the agency was looking to add to the team. Naturally, I jumped at the chance and early in 1984, signed on as an account supervisor at what was then the largest PR firm in the world. Vice chairman Stan Sauerhaft, an H&K legend, made the offer. He deposited me in the Corporate Group headed by a man named Chris Komisarjevsky. I could not have been in better hands.

Hill and Knowlton had a way of making you feel like any position there was better than the best job at another firm. Quiet, dignified and a little arrogant, it was the agency's tradition not to compete for new business. You either wanted H&K on your side or you didn't. If you decided to go with another firm, well then, you probably were not the right kind of client for H&K.

The clients on H&K's roster were blue chip and many had been with the firm for decades. Of course, the same could be said about a large segment of the staff, and as I was to learn later, the firm was starting to have to work a little harder to make the numbers each year as the average age went up and productivity went down. On the other hand, many of these lions were renowned throughout the profession and it really was an honor to get to know them and hear their stories.

Quite a few of them enjoyed a belt or three at lunchtime. I remember walking past one office and seeing its occupant poised with pen on pad, his head bent, supported by his left hand pressed against his brow. The man was obviously deep in thought. Probably wrestling with some particularly sticky problem, I thought, proud to work in a place where solving the biggest issues of the day was our stock in trade. An hour later, I walked by in the other direction and noticed that he had not moved, and there was, in those silent halls, the vague buzz of snoring emerging from the office.

#

Steve Cody and I were hard at work on the Alexander Proudfoot account. Proudfoot was a management consulting firm that had enriched its partners beyond imagination with an incredibly simple business offering: Their consultants would show up at a factory and within a month, fire 50 percent of the employees and double the productivity of those who remained. No fuss or muss for the CEO to worry about. Of course, those productivity gains only lasted for a few months until the Proudfoot guys got their engagement fee and moved on to some other unlucky site. Without whatever inducements or threats the consultants had used to stimulate productivity, output dropped like a stone. But by then, the client CEO had kicked the quarterly earnings up a notch and deposited his bonus check in the bank.

Proudfoot didn't need our help to build their business—they already had the secret formula. What they wanted was to memorialize the firm in a glossy, four-color book. Some might have called it a brochure, but the chairman would have none of it. He summoned Steve and me to a desert resort in New Mexico.

The chairman was a heavy smoker with emphysema. He alternated between puffs of a Lucky and pulls on an oxygen mask.

Cough cough. "Don't call it a brochure." *Hack hack*, "That sounds like a sales-y kind of thing."

"How about calling it a profile?" I asked.

"Oh!" *Hack hack. Slug of oxygen.* "I like that!"

Getting the profile in print occupied the better part of a year, which took the pressure off the timesheet and allowed us to hang out with some interesting people. One of the Proudfoot advisory board members was Richard Nixon, who very obligingly signed many copies of his latest tome for us to send to any of our staunch Republican colleagues (there were more than a few at H&K). Another advisory board member was Howard Samuels, one-time Undersecretary of Commerce and first-ever Commissioner of the North American Soccer League. When he died suddenly, the Proudfoot brochure—er, profile—was already printed and ready to mail. We had to go back on press to insert the words "The late" in front of Howard's name. That book could not have cost more if we had hired a monk to illuminate each copy.

(We had written most of the project on Dictaphone word processing machines, great behemoths that stored data on ten-inch floppy disks—and they really were floppy. At about that time, a colleague, named Johanna DeCourcy managed to score one of the firm's first IBM PCs. She waxed on endlessly about the PC being the wave of the future, but I didn't see what all the fuss was about. I told her so, and she looked at me with a combination of pity and disgust not unlike the look I gave my father when he said that the Beatles would be history in six months.)

Meanwhile, Steve Cody had so impressed his Proudfoot client that they offered him the job of head of public relations. Now he was my client, and while that can sometimes be a problem, in this case it was not. Steve and I remained great friends and colleagues.

# # #

Anyone who has spent a few years at a PR agency can tell you about the client that should never have been. It's an experience that scars you for life and has caused many a green pea to decamp for business school. When revenue growth slows, especially during recessions, PR firms get nervous and take on clients they know they shouldn't. It's that or start handing out pink slips. As my own experience suggests, the latter might be kinder.

One day, I was summoned to Chris Komisarjevsky's office. "I've got some great news!" he said. "We've just won a new account and I want you to lead it."

This was heady stuff for a lad with a mere four years experience under his belt. "Great!" I said. "What is it?"

"It's the city of Corpus Christi, Texas. We just met with the Corpus Christi Business Development agency and sealed the deal."

I was young, but I knew enough to ask the next question: "What's the budget?"

Chris glanced at his shoes. "Well, they signed up for the agency minimum."

H&K was so dominant among PR agencies that its leaders had established a minimum fee for client engagements—you know, to keep the riffraff out. Unfortunately, that minimum—$5,000 a month—must have been set in the 1960s and had not been revisited for decades. It was now 1984 and by any stretch of the imagination, $5,000 a month was chump change for a firm of H&K's size and resources. Hell, an account team could burn through a couple of grand just inputting their time sheets each month.

It dawned on me that the agency might be struggling, considering it had decided to take on such a small-time gig and, what's more, that I had been selected for this plum assignment. I suspected it was because I had the lowest billing rate in the Corporate group and not because of my keen insight and take-the-hill determination.

I should note that the account would have been lusted after by any small, local agency, which would have done a great job for $5K a month. But these were Texans and they seemed to like things big. And H&K was the biggest.

A week later, I flew to Corpus Christi to meet the vice-president of business development. And, unexpectedly, the head of the Port of Corpus Christi. And the head of the Convention and Visitors Bureau.

"Since we're splitting the fee three ways, I thought we should all meet right away," the VP said. Suddenly, I had not one but three clients, each of them groaning about coughing up the princely sum of $1,666 per month and making it clear that they had high expectations. Very high. Oh, and they wanted to have the fee inclusive of out-of-pocket expenses.

After our initial meeting, they took me to lunch—and proceeded to stick me with the bill!

The VP kindly drove me out to the airport, saving me a cab fare. (I briefly considered whether I should take a Greyhound bus back to New York to save money.) As we drove through the city of Corpus Christi, I noticed that all the vegetation had a brownish tinge and I asked if it was always that way. No, said the VP, we've been having a little drought. Nothing to worry about.

A couple of weeks later, the *New York Times* ran a front-page story about the terrible drought in Corpus Christi. I was summoned to Texas. As I pulled up to City Hall, I saw workers at the big hotel across the street spraying some kind of fertilizer on the grass. Only there was no grass. And it wasn't fertilizer. It was green paint. The whole city was being sprayed with green paint.

I was ushered in to meet the city manager, a burly no-nonsense type. Before I could even sit down, he waved the offending *New York Times* story under my nose and screamed—and I mean *screamed*: "YOU'RE FROM HILL AND KNOWLTON. WE PICKED YOU BECAUSE YOU'RE THE BIGGEST PR FIRM IN THE WORLD. HOW COULD YOU LET THIS GODDAM STORY HAPPEN?"

I stammered. "Well, er…you see…um …" I toyed with the idea of asking, "How could you let the goddam drought happen?" but thought better of it. We'd only been on the case for a couple of weeks and they hadn't had a chance to get used to my sense of humor.

He trained his steely eyes on me and shouted, "YOU'RE ON THIN ICE, MISTER! We just had a pool and spa convention cancel. They are going to San Diego. SAN DIEGO! We haven't had a single company call about relocating here since we hired you. WHAT ARE YOU GOING TO DO?"

I glanced out the window at the workers with their spray-can backpacks putting the finishing touches on the park at City Hall. "Let me get back to you."

From the airport, I called my buddy back at the shop. "We've got to come up with something fast. Set up a brainstorm for tomorrow."

We cooked up a dandy idea: a marketing brochure that listed all the great reasons why a company would want to be in Corpus Christi, and a roster of all the big names already there.

The tagline: "Who Put the Corp. in Corpus Christi?" We *loved* it.

The art department mocked up a dummy and we faxed it to the VP. His immediate response was quite good. "I don't recognize this company Lorem Ipsum, but overall I like the concept. The Business Development Council is meeting today—let me run it up the flagpole. In the meantime, good job."

We were elated. Until that afternoon, when he called back. We could practically *hear* him sweating over the phone.

"I need you to write a letter to me taking full responsibility for your insensitive and tasteless campaign idea!" he bleated. "The Archbishop of Corpus Christi has made a formal complaint to the mayor and the newspaper is pointing at me! I need that letter now!"

We hadn't considered the fact that "Corpus Christi" is Latin for "Body of Christ." The archbishop sat in on the Business Development Council and had gotten his mitre in a twist when he saw our sample brochure. There was no opportunity for a mea culpa, even if we'd wanted to offer one.

The VP's parting salvo: "We're invoking the 30-day termination clause in your contract, effective 30 days from today!"

It was the best news I'd received all month. If I was worried about how the client departure would affect me, I relaxed when H&K vice-chairman Stan Sauerhaft intoned, "Forget about it. [*Cue heavenly choir.*] They should never have been a Hill & Knowlton client in the first place."

# # #

Even though H&K supposedly did not compete for new business back then, it was important to the agency that prospective clients be suitably awed when they came for their first visit. To that end, the agency had invested untold sums in creating a little slideshow that prospects were obliged to sit through.

This "little slideshow" was actually a state-of-the-art multimedia extravaganza that required the simultaneous projection of 16 Kodak carousel machines. Each carousel was meticulously loaded with color slides and opaque slides so that, as the 16 churning projectors advanced from slide to slide, there would be the appearance of movement on the screen. Sadly, there really is no way to convey in writing the impact—no, doggone it, the near-majesty—of this spectacular light show. It was, of course, accompanied by "voice of God" narration and stirring music. I remember the closing words, uttered with a pomposity that still makes me cringe today: "*And through it all, for its clients and for a better world, Hill and Knowlton has been there!*"

The guy whose job it was to run the slideshow had seen it so many times that he couldn't stand to see it even once more. He barely stuck around long enough to make sure the bulbs in all the projectors were functioning. He'd flip the switch and head out to the fire escape for a smoke. Unfortunately, that meant he was not around to notice that the volume of the soundtrack had over time increased to what must have been the decibel equivalent of a jackhammer.

Time and again, prospects would emerge from the pitch black viewing room, squinting at the bright hallway lights, clearly dazed and disoriented from the visual and aural pummeling they had just been through. Looking back, it was reminiscent of news footage I have seen of bombing survivors. But somehow, it must have had the desired effect because the visitors frequently signed a contract that very day. Or maybe they just would have done anything to get out of there and onto comparatively pastoral Lexington Avenue.

Some organizations simply cannot resist a parade. One of my clients was Deloitte Haskins & Sells (now Deloitte & Touche), whose chairman, Mike Cook, was also rotating through a year as the chairman of the American Institute of Certified Public Accountants (AICPA) during the year in which it would celebrate its hundredth birthday. We were supposed to have the inside track on AICPA's PR work. But the head of communications had convinced the board that the best way to kick off a year of raucous celebrations would be to have a float in the New Year's Day Rose Bowl Parade in Pasadena, California.

I learned a thing or two about the Rose Bowl Parade as a result of Mike Cook's involvement.

- In 1986, it cost $250,000 to have a float in the parade, roughly equivalent to what the AICPA was going to spend on PR for the year, but then couldn't.

- Just because you pay the big bucks doesn't mean you have anything to do with the design of the float. That was entirely in the hands of two floral designers in Pasadena. The AICPA float could best be described as Daniel Boone with an abacus in a funeral cortege.

- "Ache-Pah" is not how you pronounce AICPA, although the parade announcers never received that memo.

- Mike Cook and his family were just radiant in buckskins and coonskin hats, waving to the crowds, although even they didn't know exactly why they were so dressed.

- Not one person I spoke to who had watched the parade could recall seeing the AICPA float.

We lost a $250,000 assignment to a parade float. I hate a parade.

33

# # # #

High above my vantage point at H&K, a clash of the titans was underway. US CEO Bob Dilenschneider had engineered a coup to push H&K's longtime chairman, Loet Velmans, into retirement. Bob took over, and something about Stan Sauerhaft just pissed him off. One day, we noticed that Stan had not been around for a few days. It might have had something to do with Bob having Stan's mahogany-paneled office cut in half and turning one side into a storage room. The word was that he'd moved to Burson-Marsteller,

Not possible, I thought. Burson had just overtaken H&K as the world's largest public relations firm, and was the Coke to H&K's Pepsi. There was no way that an H&K lifer like Stan would cross the line. (Of course, today, H&K and Burson are owned by the same company, which also owns more than a hundred other marketing, communications, and advertising companies.)

I dialed the main number of Burson and asked to be connected to Stan. A few clicks later, he was on the phone, wondering if I would like to meet for a drink.

By now I had my own PC at work and at that moment was spell-checking a letter. When the cursor got to my last name, the spell-checker was flummoxed and suggested an alternative: "Itchiness." Perfect! Itchiness was just what I was feeling. I replied to Stan's invitation: "Sure. Why not?"

Interlude:
Hey Brother, Can You Paradigm?

The fun (or should I have said unsettling) thing about paradigm shifts is that it's hard to tell when they're happening.

But I spotted one recently, and it kind of rocked my world. If your company recruits recent college graduates, chances are your new employees barely think about email—and may not use it at all. They tweet, they text, they use instant messaging. They use Facebook, Instagram and Pinterest. But the last time they dusted off their gmail accounts was to send a note back home for money. And that was only because Mom and Dad still use email. Talk about a paradigm shift!

According to Michigan State University Writing Professor Jeff Grabill, cell phones are the new pencil for Millennials. College students now rank texting as the number one form of writing and cell phones as the top writing platform.

Millennials think email is for old people. Students use it mainly to communicate with parents, professors and bosses. While they may use it, they don't value it.

I hardly need to say that email is the predominant form of communicating inside most companies. Indeed, it's getting hard to remember when it wasn't. But for today's new employees, email is no less archaic than a Smith Corona typewriter and carbon paper. (One positive thing about carbon paper—you couldn't "reply to all" by mistake. You had to really want to, and it was a lot of work.)

When I talked about a post-email world at an internal communications conference recently, there were some skeptical faces looking back at me. But afterwards, more than a few attendees told me they experienced a revelation. Suddenly they understood why their college-aged offspring responded instantly to texts, but why there could be a gap of several days before their emails were answered. *Quod erat demonstrandum.*

It's actually not such an outlandish notion, this life without email. It would hardly be the first office technology to achieve obsolescence. In an era in which most people can access a scanner, why does my business card have a fax number on it?

And platforms like Sharepoint allow secure document exchanges with colleagues and clients, without email. I correspond with my bank via its website's secure message center. I can even deposit a check by taking a picture of it with my smart phone, which suggests that in the not too distant future your children or grandchildren may ask, "What's a 'check'? And what is the 'mail' that it's supposedly in?"

To be sure, I am not predicting that Outlook will take its place in the Smithsonian next to the telegraph and carrier pigeon any time soon. But it feels like we are on the cusp of one of those paradigm-busting transitions that we usually don't see coming. Like when I noticed I no longer have ink on my fingers from reading the print edition of the *New York Times*. I have smudges on my iPad instead.

Here's what this transformation actually comes to: The basic communications model most of us use today hasn't changed much since 1886 when, in a variation of the pen being mightier than the sword, the Smith brothers quit making guns and started making typewriters. That model can be characterized as "Me talk, you listen." Communication is still largely a one-way process, unfortunately. And for all the lip service given to the desire for two-way communication, few companies have put in place the technology to facilitate and encourage up, down and sideways dialogue.

It would be great to get ahead of this post-email world. We'll have to if we want to stay relevant to our various constituents.

If your company hasn't started looking into some of the emerging platforms that can help you redefine your communications model, now's the time.

Times change. Shopping for some paper for my home printer, I came upon a product I thought I had seen the last of during the Reagan administration: carbon paper. Resisting the impulse to see if the store also stocked eight-track tape players, I paused to reflect on how much carbon paper had been a part of my early working life, and then suddenly it wasn't. I don't remember exactly when I used my last sheet of it, but if you have ever had to use the wretched stuff, I think you will agree that it lives best as a distant and not-so-fond memory.

Chapter Four

Do They Accept Amex in the Land of Oz?

I SUPPOSE THAT MANY PEOPLE who have worked at Burson-Marsteller look back at the experience 20 years later and think, "I was there for the Golden Years," but I believe that I really was there for the Golden Years. Those were the days when giants like Jim Dowling, the late Tom Mosser, Larry Snodden, Jim Lindheim, Elias "Buck" Buchwald, Al Tortorella and of course Harold Burson were running the show. I got to work alongside some of the finest professionals in the business: Mike Claes, Pat Ford, Vic Han, Diane Perlmutter and Ray O'Rourke, to name just a few.

It was an exciting time for the business. Big companies all over the world were being pummeled by takeover threats, product recalls, scandal, environmental disasters—it was a great time to be alive! Well, professionally speaking.

Increasingly, the companies beset by these problems came to Burson-Marsteller to put out their fires. Harold Burson had already emerged as the elder statesman of the profession. His counsel was sought out by the world's corporate and political leaders and he counted more than one U.S. president as a personal friend.

I remember my first real meeting with Harold. Although I had shaken hands with him when Stan took me around to meet people on my first day, several months passed before I got to see him in action.

Harold is the nicest, most cordial, humblest and smartest man I have ever known. As I write this, he still comes into the office, unless he's flying to China or Russia. At 93 years old, he wears out people half his age.

Harold has a way of cutting to the heart of the matter. The American Institute of Certified Public Accountants, my old client from H&K days, had asked us to give some thought to ways they could improve the image of accounting. As we were starting a brainstorming session, the conference room door opened and in walked Harold.

He sat down at the table and said nothing for several minutes. Finally, he spoke up. "What's the business outcome they are trying to achieve?" he asked, in his charming Southern drawl. This was greeted by silence in the conference room. "I'm sorry," he went on. "I don't mean to be obtuse, but what exactly is the AICPA trying to accomplish?" We explained the request to him and he shook his head.

"I still don't get it," Harold said, "It sounds like they just want to feel better about themselves." Heads nodded. We all waited for the magic moment when he would show us the answer, in the same fashion he had guided captains of industry and heads of state for generations.

"Well," he said, "if all this guy wants is a nice warm feeling, tell him to pee down his leg in a blue serge suit."

I loved it. I had found a home!

# # #

Burson's CEO at the time was Jim Dowling, and his vision for the PR profession was to assume a more consultative role with clients. Even as CEO, Jim prided himself on carrying a portable typewriter to client meetings and after being briefed by the client, he would ensconce himself in a client's conference room and bang out the program or press release on the spot. The words "Can I get back to you on that?" were foreign to him, and he expected his staffers to follow his lead.

Jim looked forward to the day when Burson would be viewed like the consulting firms McKinsey or Bain, despite the fact that the lion's share of our revenues came from traditional PR business. Consumer marketing, business-to-business, health care—these were the engines of our growth. But in Jim's mind, they were just a distraction.

Sadly, Jim was way ahead of his time. Most clients still looked to their PR agency for ideas and events such as "the World's Largest Postcard," and the truth is that such extravaganzas paid handsomely. Events like these on any scale had always been the bread and butter of most agencies. Young account executives often made their bones by dressing up in a costume and hijacking the *Today* show—Al Roker is well known to be a sucker for a talking ketchup bottle. And really, who isn't? And who could forget the world's largest paella, which was staged to promote a brand of dishwashing detergent?

Yet even those who enjoyed great prosperity by engineering such feats would often express a hunger to have the PR profession taken more seriously by the world's corporate leaders. And today, attend almost any convocation of PR folks and you will hear about the great strides the profession is about to make in being seen as a senior management function. The Holy Grail is "a seat at the boardroom table."

Now, I am the first to say that the deft management of an organizational crisis can burnish the image of a PR department tremendously, but fortunately for everyone concerned, those opportunities don't come along too often, and only a tiny fraction of practitioners ever get to experience the thrill and terror of wading into catastrophe and walking out the other side mostly intact.

This thought occurred to me not long ago as I perused *PRWeek*, the profession's daily publication, and saw that one of the lead stories concerned the staging of a cornhole tournament in Ohio. First I had to go to Wikipedia to look up "cornhole," which sounded vaguely salacious. Turns out it is essentially a beanbag toss. It was in the service of what I am sure is a very worthy charity, but it makes me think of the conversation three Ohio State grads might have at their tenth reunion. One notes that she is a lawyer and has been helping people facing foreclosure keep their homes. Another, a surgical nurse, describes his experience with Doctors Without Borders. And our guy recalls the cornhole tournament he just put on in Cleveland. Something feels a little…off. Still, there is dignity in any job well done, I always say. Apparently, according to *PRWeek*, the cornhole tourney was nonpareil.

The truth is that these sorts of stunts or events can be very effective in generating buzz in mainstream and new media, and sometimes that's all clients want. It's the agency's job to give it to them. I hold in high regard people who conceive of these sometimes wacky ideas and successfully pull them off. But as C-Suite credibility-enhancing activities, they are more likely to get PR firms a seat at the dinner table than at the boardroom table.

Nobody was more certain of that than Jim Dowling. As the CEO of a global agency, Jim could not turn his back completely on the marketing communications part of the business, but he focused more and more on the corporate and public affairs part. Those of us who plied that trade started to be known derisively as "Dowling's boys." We found that to be a decidedly mixed blessing. It certainly did not endear us to the rest of the agency, but it also shielded us, to a large extent, from Jim's legendary temper. Jim's fiery tantrums were notorious among the more veteran staff, but he had mellowed quite a bit by the time I got there. By then, he tended to reserve his rage for his own direct reports—the CFO, for one, had learned the fine art of dodging the electric pencil sharpener that often flew across Jim's office in the direction of his head.

# # #

Burson was always looking for new things to sell to clients. The firm had an entertainment-marketing group that somehow convinced management to invest our own money to secure the rights to a U.S. version of a London production of *The Wizard of Oz*. The big idea was that we would sell the marketing rights to the show to our clients and generate a handsome return on our investment.

Selling the show to our clients turned out to be a tough row to hoe. The rights we had purchased only gave us a short window in which to mount the show. We had no choice but to begin production and the process of securing venues without having first lined up sponsors.

At the time, I was part of a team charged with developing an executive visibility plan for a senior executive at American Express. With the global economy expanding, and more and more executives whipping out their Amex cards in exotic locales, we suggested foreign language skills as a platform that would make sense.

Before we sent the program to the client, I sent it to a one of our most senior leaders for his review. It came back to me with a note: "Looks good. Work the Wizard into it."

That was a brainstorm I won't forget.

"Okay, what if Dorothy lands in Munchkin Land and they all speak French. What would she do?"

"Okay, I see where you're going. I've got it! She takes out her Amex card and hires a translator. Can we add that to the script?"

We left the Wizard out of the proposal.

We were finally able to convince two companies to sponsor the show, which ended up bombing in a spectacular way. As *People* magazine described the ill-fated production: "The Yellow Brick Road is flanked by signs advertising Purina Dog Chow and Downy Fabric Softener. Most of the Munchkins are taller than the Tin Man. During intermission hawkers sell plastic magic wands and ruby-slipper jewelry. No, Toto, we're not in Kansas anymore. Heck, we're not even in Hollywood." Reviews were so bad that most of the venues backed out and the production soon died a quiet death.

# # #

Shell Oil was one of our bigger clients, and at the time the company had a raft of issues to keep an account team fully occupied. Most of it was pretty serious stuff, but one day my client in Houston called to say that the Western Region of Shell had agreed to be the lead sponsor of the Los Angeles Wheelchair Marathon, an annual event that coincides with the regular L.A. Marathon. The Western Region executives had blown their budget on the sponsorship, and my client agreed to fund some very limited PR activity. I think the budget he came up with was $22,000.

I called the Burson LA team and asked for their help. Howard Bragman, a true professional and delightful guy, jumped in. What would be great, he said, would be if we had a celebrity spokesperson. "Sure, it would be great," I said, "but do you seriously think that we can find anyone with any name recognition and stay within the budget?" Howard said he thought he might be able to. A couple of days later, he called and said, "I think I've got just the person."

There was an actor—kind of a B-level star—who had appeared in enough TV shows like *Cagney and Lacey* that he had some name recognition. He would be a great choice for three reasons: sadly, he had lost a leg and an arm in a motorcycle accident and was wheelchair bound; he had agreed to make an appearance for $10,000;

and he was shooting a movie in Portland, Oregon—a hop, skip and jump from L.A.

"Howard! You're a genius!" I exclaimed. I called the client and he was all for it.

The "star" had flown down to LA the day before the marathon to make an appearance at the Shell hospitality tent and pose for a few pictures with guests—the typical thing a celeb does at such an event. Evidently, he had partaken liberally of the free booze in first class and was already quite buzzed when he arrived. Once there, he started hitting the sauce hard. By the time he started posing for photos, not only was he ass-on-backwards drunk, he was mean. He started making all around him quite uncomfortable, especially when he rolled his wheelchair over backwards and required assistance to get settled again.

The next morning, he was in no shape to do much of anything, and his handlers took him back to Oregon.

Poor Howard was already stunned and depressed. The crowning moment came when an L.A. news crew interviewed the winner of the wheelchair race and he effusively praised "a big outfit like Texaco" for being a sponsor. *Um, Shell. Remember? Shell.*

# # #

When you work for a big PR firm, it should not be surprising when an assignment comes along that is a little outside the normal. Getting clients' children into the *New York Times* wedding announcements was actually a pretty common request. But putting on a high profile memorial service—that was unusual by any measure.

On January 19, 1993, quite a few years after I started at Burson, I got a call from Harold Burson.

"Chris, I have some bad news. Reg Lewis has brain cancer, and he's probably going to die today. I want you to go up to his offices and see what you can do to help with the media calls."

And there were going to be a lot of media calls. Reginald Lewis, age 50, was the wealthiest African-American businessman in the world. After graduating from Harvard Law School, he spent 17 years practicing law before starting a venture capital firm, the TLC Group. His first deal was the purchase of the McCall Pattern Company, which had been in decline for years. Reg put down a million dollars of his own money and borrowed the rest.

Reg really loved making companies better. Often, buyout firms buy a company, strip the assets, put a cattle prod into productivity and send the debt-laden carcass back out for an IPO. That wasn't Reg's style. In one year, Reg restored McCall to good health. One of his innovative ideas was to create a line of greeting cards that were manufactured with dress-pattern printing presses and other machinery that was normally idle during seasonal downtime. McCall's profitability soared, and when Reg sold the company after a couple of years, he pocketed $90 million.

I first met Reg when he hired Burson-Marsteller to handle the publicity for the TLC Group's purchase of Beatrice International Foods, in what was then the largest leveraged buyout in history. Instantly, Reg became a business celebrity around the world. He had a plane and homes in Manhattan, the Hamptons, and Paris.

Reg came to Burson because his wife, Loida, knew one of the people in my group, Rene "Butch" Meily. Butch and Loida were both Filipino by birth and had known each other in the U.S. for a while. Butch is a talented professional and a great guy. He had handled the press around the Beatrice acquisition brilliantly, and not surprisingly went to work for Reg as head of PR for TLC Beatrice.

The TLC Group's offices were at 9 West 57th Street. Butch and I sat down in Reg's office, which had a breathtaking view of

Central Park. These offices had been the former New York headquarters of RJR Nabisco, the cigarette and cookie empire. It was said that Reg's office had formerly belonged to Nabisco CEO Ross Johnson. But, the story went, Johnson had to abandon it because he couldn't get any work done—he just stared at the view. Reg, however, had more discipline.

Butch expected a ton of media calls, but he was going to handle those. He told me that he needed Burson's help for something else: a memorial service. Although I didn't quite appreciate what I was getting into, I quickly agreed.

After Reg passed away that afternoon, the family asked that the memorial service be held on Monday, January 25, just six days later. That didn't give us a lot of time, so I hurried back to my office to assemble a team. Staging a memorial service was new for me. I wasn't quite sure where to start. But my team knew a thing or two about organizing client events and sprang to work.

The first order of business was to figure out where to have the service. Reg had been raised as a Roman Catholic, so I called St. Patrick's Cathedral. The Monsignor I spoke to explained that St. Patrick's would consider a funeral, but did not permit memorial services. Since Reg's private funeral and burial were taking place over the weekend in his native Baltimore, I had to think of someplace else.

I called Riverside Church, a magnificent edifice on the Upper West Side of Manhattan. Riverside was technically a Methodist church, but famed civil rights and peace activist William Sloane Coffin, who was Riverside's senior minister, enthusiastically agreed to have the service at the church.

With the venue settled, my team began making lists: invitations, flowers, music, transportation, security, programs and a run-of-show chart that would have been the pride of any Broadway stage manager.

Our first cut of the invitation list included the most prominent African-Americans in the country. New York City Mayor David Dinkins accepted, as did the Rev. Jesse Jackson. Opera star Kathleen Battle agreed to sing, as did the Harlem Boys' Choir and Broadway star Lea Salonga. The family kept adding names to the list, and before long we had a standing room only crowd—impressive on such short notice.

Problems started popping up. Word came to us from the family that Loida wanted Kathleen Battle to sing "Amazing Grace." Ms. Battle's agent informed us that she "doesn't do Amazing Grace."

The family directed us to use a particular florist who had been the longtime supplier of floral arrangements for TLC, but it wasn't clear that this florist had the inventory to handle such a big job on such short notice.

The family asked us to use a printer in Chicago for the programs—only we had no way to be sure they would arrive in time for the service.

Early on Saturday morning, all alone in the building, the team met at 9 West 57th, and things were starting to get a little tense. Unbelievably and tragically, Butch's father had passed away the night before and Butch was now on his way to Manila. We were on our own. Another major contributor to the tension was the fact that Riverside was, well, a church and at 11 o'clock on a Sunday morning, the usual capacity crowd of worshippers was coming for normal services. That meant that we could not begin staging until the afternoon. We started going over checklists and trying to think of what we might have missed.

I paused for a smoke in the little kitchenette. I crushed out the cigarette in the wastebasket and went back to work. Shortly after, one of my team members asked, "Do you smell something burning?" I glanced at the kitchen and to my horror, smoke was coming out of it. I ran over—evidently my makeshift ashtray had caught fire. I reached for the first liquid I could find—a carafe of coffee—and poured it in, extinguishing the flames. Unfortunately, the wastebasket was not watertight, and coffee started oozing out onto the floor. I started mopping with paper towels and got the mess cleaned up, but an odor of coffee and nicotine lingered, probably for weeks. At least I hadn't burned down the building.

On Sunday, it rained. We huddled at the church doors, awaiting the end of the 11 o'clock service. Finally, the last of the worshippers left and we moved like an invasion force. The florist arrived, and our fears were confirmed. He set out a few potted plants and tied a little spray of something at the end of each pew. Riverside is a huge place and in the mammoth sanctuary, this fellow's flowers looked like lint on a suit.

A friend had put me in touch with a huge flower dealer in the Bronx, the kind of florist who can rustle up a greenhouse full of blooms on short notice. I took out my cell phone, which back then was the size of a brick, and dialed the number I had stashed in my pocket. Floral reinforcements—tens of thousands of dollars worth—arrived within a few hours, and soon the church looked like a botanical garden.

At about 7:30 that night, Kathleen Battle arrived for a run-through. She was in a foul mood (nothing unusual, I was told), screaming at her staff and mine. The Harlem Boys' Choir showed up and started singing a hymn. I was in the back of the church listening, enjoying the rare solitude of the moment, when Loida arrived with her family. I gave her my condolences and told her that Ms. Battle did not sing "Amazing Grace." I asked if she had another preference, and Loida responded, "She can sing whatever she likes."

At that moment, I turned and found myself looking into the belt buckle of a rather large man. I looked up and recognized Jean Fugett, former NFL player and CBS football commentator—Reg's half brother. He proceeded to give me one of the more severe tongue-lashings I have ever received for rudely asking Loida a question in her moment of grief. This was a little over the top in that, since Butch had departed for the Philippines, Loida had been calling me constantly, checking on details and giving us new names to invite. Well, as I said, everybody was a little tense but the stress of the previous week had left me drained and depressed. Fugett's tirade was the last straw. There was little reason to stick around, so I called a car service to take me home and went out the back door of the church to wait for it in the rain.

As the car pulled up, I remembered something I needed to tell one of my team, and bent over to reach for my briefcase. Pow! In the darkness, I slammed my forehead into the massive doorknob on the church's equally massive oak door. Immediately, blood mixed with rainwater started flowing down my face.

I tried to mop up with a car service receipt and staggered into the church with blood-smeared face. I came face to face with the Harlem Boys' Choir, whose members looked horrified at my appearance. And then I heard the impossible: Kathleen Battle's remarkable voice, singing nothing other than "Amazing Grace." I turned, got into the car and went home. My work there was done.

Monday morning was crisp and sunny. With a Band-Aid and big lump on my forehead, I arrived at the church at 7 o'clock, and everything looked terrific. Riverside has two places for a speaker: the imposing pulpit and, across the apse, an ornate lectern. We had organized the speakers to sit on the side of the apse from which they would speak. In a little room in the back of the church, I put tape on the floor with the names of the eulogists in the order in which they would sit. This would be easy. I would just greet each of the luminaries and escort them to their respective tape marks. When the procession began, everyone would be in just the right place.

By 10:30, the church had started to fill. The celebs came with their handlers, the politicians with their entourages. I greeted each and took him or her to the right spot of tape. The performers understood the tape idea immediately and stayed put; the politicians, not so much. Mayor Dinkins arrived and I took him to his spot. Pointing at the tape, he asked, "What's this?" I explained, and he frowned and grunted. But just then, Jesse Jackson strode in.

I said, "Good morning, Reverend Jackson. If you'll just follow me…"

"Unless it's to a men's room, I'm not following you anywhere," he replied. I showed him the way.

Back in the "green room," as we were calling it, Mayor Dinkins was looking displeased. He had figured out that the line of people he would lead would be at the lectern. "I usually speak from the pulpit," he said.

I explained that members of the family would be the main speakers in the pulpit. The mayor shook his head. "I have never spoken at Riverside from anywhere but the pulpit," he said with annoyance. It was just five minutes to show time.

My team saved the day, reorganizing the lines and giving the mayor what he wanted. He was now in the other line, ahead of Jesse Jackson, who didn't seem to care.

At a few minutes past 11, the music started and the procession began. I sat down in the back to watch. Out of the corner of my eye, I saw someone at the church door. It was Al Sharpton. The only problem was he was not on the invitation list. Mayor Dinkins' security chief walked up to him, pointed to a chair near mine and quietly said, "My way or the highway." Rev. Sharpton nodded and took a seat.

The service went off flawlessly, and when it concluded, the procession reversed and the dignitaries walked down the aisle and out the door to the street. As Jesse Jackson reached the threshold, Al Sharpton appeared out of nowhere, grabbed Rev. Jackson's hand, held it high and walked out with him onto the steps of the church, where dozens of reporters and cameras awaited. The next day, that was the picture that ran in the *New York Times*.

Interlude:
Lessons from the Whiteboard

For the last several years, I have had a whiteboard in my office on which I have written a number of adages that have come to mean something to me over the years. The list currently numbers 24. It changes now and then, with new entries supplanting older ones that have not aged as well as I thought they might. So it's always a work in progress, but here are a couple that have endured.

The first is a quote from Edward R. Murrow, the legendary newsman who pioneered broadcast journalism:

> If you're going to invite me to the crash,
> please invite me to the takeoff.

For many corporate communications leaders, this plea has great resonance. Firefighters will tell you that they would much rather prevent a fire than run headlong into one. Too often, the PR team gets a call after the flames are licking at the rafters or, to use Murrow's analogy, the plane has begun its downward spiral. No matter how nimble the response, damage is inevitable.

Obviously, the sooner the PR team knows what may be coming down the pike, the greater the possibility of mitigating the impact—or even eliminating it. Running a proposed initiative by the PR folks is always a good idea—it may cause management to rethink, or even possibly abandon, the new plan before somebody gets hurt.

Item 19 on my whiteboard provides a clue as to why this strategy is ignored all too often:

> Every problem began as a solution.

By definition, unintended consequences tend to catch us unawares. What seems like a perfect and elegant solution to a problem may instead create an even bigger problem. But often, people can only see the upside of the solution, saying to themselves, "No need to run this by the PR team. I mean, what could go wrong?" Entire careers in crisis response have been launched with those words.

Item 20:

> You can observe a lot by watching.

If that sounds like Yogi Berra, that's because it was indeed a classic Yogi-ism. But unlike many of his memorable lines, there is profundity (almost certainly unintended) underlying the words. Talk less, watch and listen more. Watching and listening are for most people passive activities that—quite literally—you can perform without thinking. And that's exactly the point. Learn not only to watch but to see, not just to listen but to hear. Ask yourself why a person said what he or she said in the way that s/he did. What was left unsaid? Was the speaker looking at you or away? Do you think you are getting the whole story? This is especially important at the outset of a relationship, when both parties are trying to size each other up.

Last item:

> Before you criticize someone, walk a mile in his shoes.
> That way, when you criticize him, you'll be a mile away and
> you'll have his shoes.

No explanation necessary.

Chapter Five

The Monk, the Concorde and the Second Coming

THE LATE 1980S, WHEN I was still early in my tenure with Burson, brought a huge number of mergers and acquisitions, and we went after that business aggressively. It was very profitable and our fees (tiny next to those of bankers and lawyers) were wrapped into the deal expenses. There was never any client pushback.

It could be grueling 24/7 work and for several years, I never celebrated Memorial Day, the Fourth of July or Labor Day with my family. Three-day weekends were ideal for closing a deal.

There was so much money flying around that it made things a little tense from time to time, especially among the bankers who had such gigantic fees riding on a given deal. Even guys (and they were almost all men) who were friendly and pleasant under normal circumstances became tigers during a takeover.

My baptism in M&A work came on a Saturday night, when Stan Sauerhaft called me at home. We had been selected to work for Harcourt Brace Jovanovich, the textbook publisher, which was being attacked by British media magnate Robert Maxwell. Stan had a golf date the next day so he dispatched me to Harcourt's offices in

Orlando in his place. I met the lead banker from First Boston, who was only interested in slinging mud at Maxwell.

"Get me a story in the *Financial Times* that rubs shit all over Maxwell's fat face!" he demanded. I was feeling a little out of my league, but fortunately, Burson had a superb global network, and although it was early Sunday evening in the U.K., I called Terence Fane-Saunders, the head of our London office. I started explaining what I wanted to do, but he cut me off, saying, "I'm terribly sorry, but Mike Horton has just died and I must run back to the hotel." I had no idea what he was talking about.

I was so new at Burson, I didn't even know who Mike Horton was. He was, in fact, a much-beloved senior executive in Burson's European operations. Over the next few days, the details of Mike's demise became tabloid fodder in a very big way.

Burson's worldwide management team was meeting in London. At the end of the day's session, the meeting broke up and people went back to their hotel rooms to freshen up for dinner. Except Mike, who walked over to the nearby Churchill Hotel. There, waiting for Mike, was the husband of a woman with whom Mike was having an affair. The husband began to make a scene and Mike suggested they relocate to the husband's room. The husband demanded that Mike end the affair. Apparently Mike refused, which led to the husband hitting Mike over the head, first with a bottle of mineral water, then with a bottle of gin. Finally, he grabbed a small penknife he used for sharpening pencils and repeatedly stabbed Mike in the neck with it.

Back in Orlando, I was trying to figure out how to explain to the banker that not only were the London media consumed with this sensational story and completely uninterested in Maxwell, the story they *were* reporting rather prominently featured Burson-Marsteller! I decided to hold back on that for a while, and on Monday night I flew back to New York.

By mid-week, the media team at Burson's London office had absorbed the impact of Mike's death as best they could and graciously accepted the challenge of planting some Maxwell mud. I could tell that this team was really good, but I was still surprised when, only a few days later, the London team called to say that a story was going to run in the *FT* the next day. I triumphantly called the banker to let him know the good news, and he demanded to know what the story was going to say. I, of course, had no clue. "Find out now!" he yelled.

This was 1987. There was no Internet as we know it. I had to call "Information" in London to get the number of the *FT*. It was already midnight there, but I made the call anyway. I wasn't sure what I was going to ask if someone answered. I let the phone ring about 30 times and was about to hang up when there was a click-click and someone picked up.

"'Ello!" said the voice, in a thick Cockney accent.

"Hello! Is this the *Financial Times*?" I asked.

"It is. It's the loading bay."

"The loading bay?"

"That's what I said, didn't I?"

I never did find out why the phone was set to ring in the loading bay, but I could not believe my good fortune. I explained that I needed to get a copy of the paper right away and the voice told me that he and his crew were at that moment loading the papers onto trucks for delivery in the morning. I asked if I could send someone over to pick up a copy.

"Sorry, Guv. Not allowed."

My mind was racing. "Do you suppose that you could read a story to me, right now?"

"I suppose I could," he replied. I told him the story was about Robert Maxwell. He said, "Right! There it is, right on the front page. Shall I start?"

"Please!" I said, reaching for pen and paper.

He started reading the story, pausing every now and then to ask, "Got that, Guv?" At one point he stopped and exclaimed, "I don't think Mr. Maxwell is going to like this story, not one bit... heh heh heh."

He finished his recitation and I thanked him profusely. "Right then, cheers!" he said as he hung up.

I called the banker and read my notes to him, grinning because I knew he would be awed by my initiative and resourcefulness. When I finished, he said, "Thanks," and hung up.

#

The nice thing about M&A work was that if you had the contacts in the banking and legal community, the business just came to you—there was never a shoot-out between agencies. Too bad the rest of the business was not like that.

Unlike at Hill and Knowlton, the hyper-competitive pursuit of new business was the ever-present yin to our client-service yang. At all times, somewhere within the agency's 13 floors at 230 Park Avenue South, there was an account team scrambling to meet a presentation deadline. As difficult as the creative ideation could be, the actual assembly of the necessary presentation books, display boards, souvenirs and slide copy was exhausting, and the last-minute rehearsals late at night did not help.

And you did all this knowing that if your team won the business, there was a good chance that the client's *real* budget would never cover the big idea they'd come to hear. "We don't want to tell you the budget because we don't want to limit your thinking," prospects would invariably say. "If it's a big enough idea, we'll find the money." But of course, they never found the money. Even if we could have guaranteed that we could make the granite presidents of Mt. Rushmore sing a barbershop rendition of their latest commercial jingle, they still would never have found the money.

The pursuit of large accounts often resembled the run-up to the Invasion of Normandy. And without question, the biggest pain point in preparing for a new business pitch was making the dreaded 35mm slides.

If you started your first job after the mid-1990s, you have never known life without PowerPoint.

The PR business was quick to embrace PowerPoint because it solved so many of the problems that attended earlier technologies such as 35mm slides and overhead transparencies. It gave us the ability to edit presentations on the fly. But this was a double-edged sword as it often led to staff making radical changes to the "deck" even as the prospective client was settling in at the conference table. While it was wonderful to be able to fix a potentially devastating typo—such as misspelled client names or the catastrophic "Pubic Relations"—before it appeared in six-inch letters on a screen, sometimes the changes were more extensive. There was no chance to rehearse the modifications, often leading to desperate "Is-this-your-slide-or-mine?" telepathy attempts across a darkened room. It was almost worse when the changes came the day before. The ability to edit or completely re-write a presentation at the last minute often meant staying up into the wee hours to make changes, rehearse them, make more changes, re-rehearse them, ad infinitum. It's no wonder that so many pitch teams ended up looking glassy-eyed and haggard.

Which is not to say that the 35mm slides of days gone by were a treat. If you discovered an error in a slide at the last minute, you had two choices: Either discard the slide and hope to remember its main point or leave the slide in, rocket through it, and hope nobody noticed the mistake.

Every PR person has a story about his or her worst new business nightmare. I am pleased that I have had very few truly spectacular crash-and-burns, but one particular new business pitch stands out.

I was part of a Burson team that flew out west to make a big corporate positioning pitch to Boeing, with whom we had worked on an abortive takeover threat by T. Boone Pickens. The company's vice president of PR suggested that we come out in time to run through the presentation with his team before showing it to the CEO. We were scheduled to present to the CEO at 2 o'clock, right after lunch.

We met with the PR team and started going through the slides. The VP had a lot of suggestions. "You can lose the Asia stuff, this is a U.S. campaign." I started pulling slides out of the carousel. "Don't need help in DC, we've got that covered already." More slides pulled. Then, "Let's move that section to the back." By the time we were done, we had reduced and reorganized the presentation considerably. The VP then leapt from his chair and said, "Okay, let's go to lunch." He started out the door of the conference room.

I was scrambling to get the slides in the right slots in the carousel and when I thought I had them all set, ran after the group as they were sitting down in the executive dining room.

Lunch dragged on and before I knew it, it was ten minutes to two. The next thing I knew, we were back in the conference room as the CEO strode in with a couple of spear-carriers in tow.

The lights were dimmed, and we began. Stan Sauerhaft had accompanied us for the pitch and he led off. Stan did not care for rehearsing and hadn't given a lot of thought to what he was supposed to say, so he read from our written proposal. Since it was somewhat dark in the room, his delivery was a little spotty. He stood with the proposal angled to try to catch some light from the projector and said, "Therefore, we are…uh…placed…no, pleased to…prevent… er, no that should be present …." The clients sat expressionless in the darkness.

At long last, it was my turn. I thought I might be able to salvage the mess. I was very proud of a series of "build" slides I had made— these are the ones that start with a slide with one bullet point on it, the next has two bullet points, and so on. To my horror, when I got to my first build slide, I saw that it had five bullet points! The next slide had four! My beloved build slides were in reverse order.

My right leg began to move forward and back as if I were a Rockette on a kick line, as I valiantly tried to move through the slides as if nothing were wrong. In the process, my leg became ensnarled in the cord that attached the remote control to the projector. I willed my leg to go vertical and then somehow yanked the projector so that it ended up aimed right into my eyes.

Momentarily stunned by the blinding light, I started clearing my throat. My colleagues later told me that I sounded like a cat coughing up a hairball. The final indignity came when the CEO himself got up to get me a glass of water. His gracious gesture was the last straw. I gave up, passing the remote control on to one of my colleagues, and retreated to the darkest corner of the room.

After the pitch, the VP escorted us out. His parting words rang in our ears as we set out for the airport. "Thanks, I guess. We'll call you." And that was the last we ever heard from him.

# # #

But new business pitches were not the only way to distinguish yourself with abject failure. You could also do that in a normal day's work. Such was the sad case of Anchor Savings Bank, a local New York institution.

Anchor was one of my first clients at Burson. The bank was best known for its campy, homemade commercials featuring the CEO, Don Thomas, and his wife. For a few years, all was well, but then one day, the bank announced that it was going to launch an initial public offering. We had quite a bit of experience with IPOs and set to work. Happily, the IPO was a fantastic success. Mr. Thomas made a fortune and retired; shortly after, a new CEO was named. We wanted to impress the new guy with our media relations savvy and crafted a poetic press release announcing his arrival. The headline read, "Anchor Savings Bank Appoints James Large as CEO" and after securing the requisite client approvals, we sent it off to one of the press release distribution services.

A couple of hours later, the release went out on US 1—the PR equivalent of carpet bombing—with the headline, "Anchor Savings Bank Appoints Large CEO." The next morning, the clips started rolling in. The most memorable was in the *New York Post*, known for its punning headlines. Theirs was, "A Big Man for a Big Job."

I called the newswire service rep and asked, "Why the hell did you change my headline?"

"We use the *AP Style Manual*," the rep replied. "It says to use only the last name in a headline. And the story got great pick-up!"

"It sure did," I yelped. "More coverage than I ever wanted! Please do not send us a bill!" Good thing, too, as we were the ex-agency by the end of the day.

# # #

Sometimes new business begins with a request for proposal and a long, drawn out process during which many agencies are asked to present their best thinking for a potential client. Each agency may invest tens of thousands of unreimbursed dollars in these pitches, but only one agency can win.

On the other hand, sometimes a potential client just falls into your lap. Often, this turns out to be not such a good thing.

A few years into my tenure at Burson, one of my buddies stuck his head into my office doorway.

"Listen," he said. "I know we were supposed to go to lunch today, but we just got a call about a huge new business opportunity. The prospect wants to meet immediately—today—and Buck wants me at the meeting."

Elias "Buck" Buchwald was a vice chairman and the first person Harold Burson hired after founding the firm. He is incredibly smart and devilishly funny to this day, and he delighted in seeing the irony in a situation—often when nobody else did. His office was adorned with a huge rack of pipes—corn cob pipes, briar pipes, Meerschaums, you name it.

It was the early 1990s, and the country was in the midst of yet another major recession. The agency was scrambling for new business. We welcomed all comers as long as the prospect's credit report wasn't actually smoldering and the company passed the mirror test, the one eighteenth-century doctors used to determine if a patient was still breathing! But this opportunity had come up so suddenly that the agency hadn't had time to do even minimal due diligence.

Of course I understood, I told him, and wished him luck. I went out for a sandwich, wondering about the potential new client.

A few hours later, my buddy returned. He slumped into a chair in my office.

"How'd it go?" I asked.

"Well, I would have to say it was one of the most memorable meetings I've ever been in."

I leaned back in my chair. "Do tell."

The prospect had been whisked into Buck's office. The agency team bristled with anticipation. What was so important it couldn't wait even one day? Was it a product recall? A jail-bound CEO? A chemical spill? It *had* to be huge.

After a round of introductions, the prospect—Mr. Goldthwaite—wasted no time.

"Thank you for meeting with me on such short notice. There is much work to be done, and we don't have a lot of time. First, I need to ask about your credentials. Tell me about your experience handling major events, the kind of event that would attract worldwide media attention."

Buck smiled broadly. "Big events are the hallmark of this agency," he boasted. "Just last month we orchestrated the awards ceremony for the Winter Olympics, with a laser light show, fireworks, music, the whole shebang. It was broadcast around the world! So how can we help you?"

"I am aware of your Olympics work, it's one of the reasons I called you," said Mr. Goldthwaite. "But I'm talking about a press conference. Can you manage one that would have hundreds or thousands of reporters in attendance? Where would you stage it, and how long would it take to get it ready?"

After the slightest hesitation, Buck responded. "You're in luck. Sitting right here is our director of media relations. He can give you plenty of examples of big press conferences we've staged for our clients. Ben?"

Ben delivered a couple of brilliant case studies. (In new business pitches, the case studies are always brilliant.) And he wrapped up by assuring Goldthwaite there was nothing he could throw at the agency that we couldn't handle.

Goldthwaite nodded. "I will also have to insist this engagement be handled by your most senior agency personnel, including the CEO. Nothing less will do. I need people with experience and maturity, people with gravitas."

Buck assured Goldthwaite that the agency always put the best people on every engagement, and this would be no exception. "But now I must ask, Mr. Goldthwaite, what, exactly, is this event going to be?"

Goldthwaite rose and shut the office door. He sat back down and looked directly at each person for a moment.

"What I am about to reveal must stay in this room. Nobody outside these walls can know anything about it until we are ready. I need to know that you will maintain absolute confidentiality. If anyone else learns about our work prematurely, we could lose control of everything. Do I have your solemn word?"

Again, he looked each person in the eye. Each person murmured agreement.

He leaned forward. Buck leaned in as well. Their heads were almost touching.

"The date of the event is April twenty-third. On that day, we the people of Earth will witness the second coming of Jesus Christ."

A long silence followed. Finally, Buck sat back and took a pull on his Meerschaum pipe and asked, "And?"

Shocked, Goldthwaite asked, "What do you mean 'and'?"

"I mean," said Buck, "if you want the press to turn out, we usually need some kind of news hook to work with."

\# \# \#

In the fullness of time, certain clients turn out to be difficult and dreadful; others turn out to be delightful to work with and provide lovely memories. One of my favorite Burson clients was Lloyd's of London. Lloyd's was renowned for its willingness to take on all kinds of outsized risks—major catastrophes, environmental disasters, that sort of thing. They also were willing to take on what some would say were frivolous risks—such as insuring Irish stepdancer Michael Flatley's legs for $47 million—and enjoying lots of great publicity in the bargain.

Lloyd's is not a conventional insurance company *per se* but an insurance market. On the large underwriting floor at the Lloyd's building at One Lime Street, underwriters sit in boxes waiting for Lloyd's brokers to come make their pitches. Suppose a broker wanted to line up insurance against a particular calamity. Depending on the potential exposure, it is unlikely that any single underwriter would assume that risk alone. So an underwriter might sign on for 2 percent of the risk. The broker would then move on to the next box and the next until he had covered 100 percent of the risk.

The underwriters ran what are called syndicates. The syndicates comprise corporations and well-heeled individuals who put up substantial sums of cash to join the syndicate. At that time, individual members, known as "names," had to put up at least $250,000 to join. And they did so by participating in an unusual process. Each name was required to visit One Lime Street for a meeting with Lloyd's officials. The purpose of the meeting was to explain in great detail the implications of becoming a name.

Historically, the investment returns on these syndicates had been enormous. A name could reap a 50 percent return in a year or two. But each name needed to also understand and agree to another fact of investment life. Sometimes syndicates did not do so well. If they did not, the name's exposure did not end with the initial investment. The name would be on the hook for a proportionate share of the entire loss, even if it resulted in bankruptcy. The only things that were safe were the tools of your trade. After seizing the manor house, the cars, the gaming guns and the family dog, Lloyd's didn't want to leave a name unable to scratch out some wretched kind of a living. "We take it all, right down to their cufflinks," one executive told me. "Of course, that has *almost never* happened."

Most names were so intoxicated by the desire to drop the fact that they were a name in cocktail conversation, they probably didn't take the warning seriously. And the vast majority of them did quite well.

However, in the early 1990s, there were a number of syndicates that had underwritten asbestos claims in the U.S. As litigation expenses and jury awards began to accelerate, a number of underwriters began to sweat. It was said (although never proven) that as a result, these underwriters colluded with U.S.-based brokers to sign up new names. "Recruit to dilute" was the mission, meaning to spread the liabilities across a bigger pot of money.

A number of high-profile executives and boastful oil tycoons were seduced into becoming names, unaware that they were being suckered into joining syndicates already facing massive losses. When the extent of their own likely losses became clear, these new names did what any red-blooded American would do—they sued. These suits generated a lot of nasty press coverage in the U.S. and the U.K.

For the most part, the cases were settled out of court. That's about the time we were brought in—to try to manage the U.S. press coverage around the settlement and attempt to buff up Lloyd's image.

A couple of us flew over to meet with management. One Lime Street was a startling building, designed by noted British architect Richard Rodgers, and one either reveled in its novelty or loathed it completely. I counted myself in the latter group and I was in good company. Prince Charles was so disgusted with One Lime that he launched a campaign against ugly buildings in the U.K., with the Lloyd's building as the poster child. Charles was quoted in the press as saying, "You have to give this much to the Luftwaffe. When it knocked down our buildings, it didn't replace them with anything more offensive than rubble." Good one, Charlie!

At One Lime, everything that was supposed to be on the inside was on the outside. The bathrooms were bolted onto the side of the building and were constructed of stainless steel, wall to wall. It gave a whole new meaning to "going to the can." When the building first opened, one of the tabloids ran a cartoon of a car as if designed by Rodgers. It had the engine, seats and window rollers on the outside, and a bumper protruding from within. The cartoon was displayed with honor in the Lloyd's pressroom. At least they had a sense of humor.

Our first meeting—to which we were escorted by Peter Hill, Lloyd's charming head of PR at the time—was with Sir David Rowland and Peter Middleton, respectively, chairman and president of the firm. Sir David was as reserved and stoic as you would imagine a British banker to be, but Peter was a former monk who rode to work on a motorcycle. He was never without a cigarette dangling from his lips and (as we later learned) appreciated a fine wine. Both seemed deeply concerned about Lloyd's reputation in the U.S. and were pleased to welcome us.

After the meeting, we went to a conference room for a working lunch with two suspender-clad executives. As we walked into the conference room, we were taken aback by the spread they had laid out. While we in the States would order a platter of deli sandwiches and Diet Cokes for a meeting, here there were two different steam trays and a mountain of salads, cookies, cakes…and several bottles of French wine, both red and white. The executives greeted us warmly and offered us a glass, but we were so jet-lagged that we didn't dare risk falling asleep. "Suit yourselves," one of them said as he reached for a bottle of sauvignon blanc. The other popped open a nice claret. During the course of lunch, we learned all about the intricacies of the Lloyd's market, and also just how much wine two guys could put away in 90 minutes and still go back to work. Later, Peter Hill gave us an amused look as we described the meeting, and said that Lloyd's had the distinction of being the last firm in the City where one could expect to get thoroughly potted at lunch with no consequences.

After a couple of days of briefings, we flew home and got to work. We put together a plan and arranged for a videoconference to present it. Four of us sat at a conference table in New York, and Sir David and Peter sat at one in London. The box that we used to control the video camera and that picked up our voices was on the table in front of us.

As I made a point about media outreach, one of my colleagues set her coffee mug down on the table next to the control box. Both Sir David and Peter winced. I knocked my knee into the table while crossing my legs and they instantly looked stricken. Evidently, the sound level on their side of the ocean was set one notch below "thunderclap" and when I dropped my pen on the table, they recoiled as if they were being physically assaulted. Someone said something funny and we all laughed out loud; Peter and David looked nauseous. Finally, the hand and arm of an otherwise unseen Peter Hill reached into the picture and turned down the volume. I am sure Sir David considered Mr. Hill a peer from then on.

We needed a spokesperson in New York and Peter Middleton volunteered. He came over the night before our first round of interviews and we took him to dinner. We asked him how his flight had been.

"Well, it was rather a surprise," he said. Apparently, Peter had been upgraded to the Concorde and shortly after take-off, the flight attendant had told him that the Captain had seen his name on the passenger list and wondered if he was the Peter Middleton of Lloyd's and if so, would he care to visit the flight deck?

It turns out that the Captain was a name.

"Now, as you can imagine," Peter explained, "one always wonders if the person is a 'happy' name or an 'unhappy' name, but the only way to find out was to go up front. I followed the flight attendant onto the flight deck. The captain introduced himself, saying he just wanted to say how satisfied he was with his membership at Lloyd's."

Peter thanked him and commented on the amazing view of the earth's curvature from the Concorde. The captain then asked if Peter would like to sit down. Wild man-motorcyclist-ex-monk

Peter jumped at the chance—and in no time, had switched places with the co-pilot.

"Then," he went on, "the captain asked if they could get me anything, and I said that I had left my glass of wine at my seat. The captain raised his eyebrows and then shrugged and said to the flight attendant, 'Oh, why not?' "

"So there I was, ensconced in the co-pilot's seat with a glass of wine and a view very few people have ever had."

I asked Peter how long they let him sit there. He fired up a Marlboro, blew out a big smoke ring, and calmly replied: "Until we parked at the gate at JFK."

I don't know how many British and American aviation laws were broken that day, but that was just the sort of thing that would happen to Peter Middleton. I was very sorry to read of his death in April 2014. He was truly a shining star.

# # #

A few years after I started at Burson, the head of the New York office, Tom Mosser, convened a group of people to consider some quality-of-life issues the staff was experiencing. He asked the group to get back to him in a month or so, and the group began to hold regular meetings. Tom didn't sit in on these sessions—he just wanted the final recommendations.

Finally, the group had assembled a list of issues and requested a meeting with Tom. Tom asked a few members of the management committee to sit in as well, including me. We gathered in a conference room and the group's appointed spokesperson began with a recitation of the issues the group had identified.

The young woman who had been appointed as the spokesperson dove in.

"Everybody is working crazy hours," she began. "We have to do our client work all day and then work on new business after hours. Weekends in the office are common. Our technology is way behind the times and almost nobody has a PC. The cubicles deprive everyone of privacy. Supervisors don't know how to manage. Promotions and raises come too slowly. Our clients treat us like slaves. We lowball the fees for our projects and then get yelled at for going over budget. The amount of unbillable time we have to spend producing client invoices is growing. The copy machines don't work half the time. And the carpets are stained and disgusting."

The head of HR was present, and she was furiously taking notes and saying encouraging things like, "Mmm" and "I see." Tom listened attentively, nodding and asking a few questions. When the litany of problems was finally complete, Tom said, "Thank you for putting so much effort into this project. You have identified some important concerns. What are your recommendations?"

The designated spokesperson looked Tom in the eye and said, "Casual Fridays."

Tom responded, "That's it? Nothing else?"

The group nodded as one. Tom tried again.

"Let me see if I have this right. You are working too hard, you have demanding clients, our technology is in the Stone Age and you don't like working conditions in the building?" he asked. "And the solution to all of this is Casual Fridays? Do I have that right?"

Another group nod.

"Well," he replied, "that is certainly not what I was expecting."

I personally was dumbfounded. To his credit, Tom maintained a straight face, although I knew he wanted to burst out laughing.

"Thank you again for your valuable input," Tom said. "I'll raise it at the next management committee meeting and we'll get back to you."

For the record, I didn't notice any particular improvement in any of the many issues the group had raised as a result of the new Casual Fridays.

In the typical Burson way, such changes had to be accompanied by rules, which appeared to have been modeled after the dress code of a prep school. No jeans, no tank tops, no tee shirts. No skorts, no shorts, no open-toe sandals. One employee, Lauren Letellier (who I married a few years later, possibly because of this line), scornfully joked: "Show me a closed-toe sandal, and I'll show you a clog."

The early 1990s brought a horrific recession that forced the agency to start making unprecedented layoffs. I was one of the four members of the management committee, and we were charged with coming up with a plan to cut $2 million from our payroll—a daunting figure given the piss-poor pay most PR agency staff pulled down. After a long and heated philosophical debate, we decided that the fairest way to make the number was to take a hard look at the salaries and productivity of our most senior executives.

With heavy hearts, we presented our recommendations to Larry Snodden, who had taken over from Jim Dowling as CEO. But Larry felt that we should take a kinder, gentler approach. We would offer everybody in the firm a voluntary separation package, with an enhanced severance package: 25 percent above our standard package for staff with fewer than ten years' service, and 50 percent above for those with more than 10 years. I didn't have a good feeling about this, especially when HR revealed that the formal name of the initiative would be the "Career Transition Program." God, do I love a spinmeister!

When the program's deadline arrived, the vast majority of volunteers not only had fewer than 10 years' service, most had fewer than five. The severance premium for most of them amounted to about a day's pay but for dozens of these disillusioned young professionals, this was all it took to spur applications to law school or an

MBA program. Unbelievably, now we were looking at staff shortages, and the deadwood we had hoped to clear out was still there.

It got so bad that laughing was the only coping skill we could muster. Our finances would not allow for one of the lavish Burson holiday parties of the past; we had to do something in-house. We had planned something special. Six of us conspired to provide a little comic relief, and in total secrecy, we wrote and produced a musical revue lampooning life at Burson to the tunes of Broadway standards. Our production team discreetly called in all their favors and we were able to set up a stage and lights in our biggest conference room, far away from the party floor.

A guerilla marketing campaign the morning of the big day led to a full house for the first show, and word of mouth brought in a standing-room-only crowd for a second show. We all thought we might be putting our jobs in jeopardy, but "Forbidden Burson" was a smash, and before long, we were invited to take it on the road to our DC office.

As fun as "Forbidden Burson" was, it was also a tipping point for me. I knew that I was burned out from the stress of the last few years and that I was growing more cynical than I cared to admit. After eight years, it was time to move on again.

I called PR search guru Bill Heyman and he said, "Ya know, I think I've got just what you're looking for."

Interlude:
Could You Land a Plane?

A fellow communications practitioner once said to me, "I may be the PR guy, not the CEO, but in an emergency I could land the plane."

What did he mean by that? He meant that he understood enough about how his company worked—how it made and spent money, innovated, manufactured, marketed, and sold—that if called upon in an emergency, he could manage the company's operations, at least for a while.

By the time you've become a senior communications professional, you ought to be able to land the plane. I'm not suggesting communicators must master engineering, chemistry, information technology or the law. But whether you are asked for a plan to launch a new product or are ripped away from your desk to help the company manage a crisis, your recommendations had better be rooted in a deep understanding of how things work where you work.

Outside consultants can easily fall into this trap. Even if they bring relevant experience from work with clients in the same industry, some of their recommendations are bound to go wide of the mark until they really get to know a client's company. (In fairness, I recognize that in many cases, the most valuable counsel agencies provide is valuable precisely because it is unsullied by the "why-it-won't-work-here" syndrome.)

And even insiders can be myopic—so focused on the intricacies of their particular discipline they may never fully comprehend how things work out in the field or in the plant. Some companies rotate executives from one function to another. These tours of duty can mean that an engineer who has spent time in the PR department will understand the importance of a timely response to a media query (especially in a crisis) and thus be more helpful to the PR team.

Some advice I would give to anyone at any stage of her or his career:

If you work for a company that makes stuff, ask if you can take a tour of one of the manufacturing facilities. Talk with the plant manager about its operation and maintenance. Find out what kinds of problems he or she has to grapple with.

Ask if you can shadow a sales professional on a few calls. Learn the dynamic between sales and procurement.

See if you can sit in on some planning meetings with marketing, sales, operations and management teams—people you might otherwise never get to meet.

There is no substitute for walking in someone else's steel-toed shoes. Some fast food chains regularly put middle and senior executives behind the counter to experience dealing with customers and stressed-out employees. Communication leaders might want to think about paying for agency staff to have some of these experiences, too, as it will make their insights all the deeper.

Become a voracious consumer of the trade press that covers your company. Understand the issues facing your industry and how your competitors manage them; it will make you a valuable counselor to management.

And for heaven's sake, read *The Wall Street Journal.* Every day. It will provide context for what is happening to and in your industry and in the economy in general. If you can squeeze in time for the *Financial Times, Fortune* and *The Economist,* so much the better.

The more you know about your company, the more likely that you'll sense when something is not quite right and call it to the attention of those who need to know before it becomes a crisis.

I actually did learn to fly a plane and it has taught me a lot of things, but none more important than to stay alert at all times. Things can happen fast in the air; the broader your view, the more likely you'll see trouble coming early and get out of its way. Good career advice, too.

Chapter Six

When It Absolutely, Positively Lands Upside Down

THE LOBBY OF THE NEWS Building at 220 E. 42nd Street in New York is one of the most impressive lobbies in the city. The centerpiece is a giant globe recessed into the floor and embedded in the floor are brass plates that have labels such as "Buenos Aires 5,277 miles." The building, once home to the *New York Daily News*, is an art deco masterpiece. The façade appears in some of the later *Superman* movies as the home of *The Daily Planet*. It became my new work home in July 1995, when I moved to Ketchum.

Ketchum was everything Burson was not: youthful, upbeat and making money. The cynicism that had taken root at Burson was nowhere to be found at Ketchum. Quite a few senior people at Ketchum had left Burson to go there, including Rob Flaherty, now the CEO. I think they must have made a vow not to let Ketchum go the way of Burson. (Today's Burson-Marsteller seems to be a vibrant, exciting place, but in the mid-'90s, it just wasn't a fun place to be.)

In fact, not long after I started at Ketchum, I lent a copy of "Forbidden Burson" to Rob, then the head of the New York office. The next day he gave it back. "Very funny," he said. "But please never show this to anyone at Ketchum. I don't want anyone here to know it can get that bad."

One of the reasons Ketchum has succeeded in good times and bad is because of its management continuity. Burson had run through four CEOs in eight years, whereas Ketchum had had the same team in place for those eight years and for the nine I was there—and pretty much ever since. Say what you want about fresh blood being healthy for an agency, stability in the executive ranks gives people one less thing to worry about.

The other result of a long-tenured team was a culture that was almost palpable. There were Ketchum People and there were Not-Ketchum People. The agency worked hard to avoid hiring the latter, and was generally quick to expel them when mistakes occasionally occurred. So it was all the more strange that they hired *me* and that I stayed for as long as I did.

Ketchum had a superb reputation as a consumer and business-to-business powerhouse. It had won more industry awards in these areas than any other agency and its account leadership was the best in the business. But they had never really been able to get a classic corporate group up and running—at least not one that could credibly compete with Burson and Hill and Knowlton, not to mention deal shops like Kekst and Abernathy McGregor. There was a group called the Corporate Group, but it was really a collection of B2B accounts and a smattering of financial services.

My job was to shore that up, and on paper I had the credentials to do it. But I had just spent eight years at Burson, where we were encouraged to take ourselves very, very seriously. If Burson was a cocktail party, Ketchum was a beer blast. Looking back, I consider that to be a compliment to Ketchum.

# # #

About six months after I started, Rob Flaherty called to tell me that the person who had been leading the FedEx account was leaving the agency. He asked if I would take over. I was thrilled. I was and still am awed by the company, which had become an icon of global business only 23 years after its founding.

FedEx had some of the best toys a guy could imagine, like MD-11s, MD-10s and Airbus 300s—the massive, three-engine jets that are the workhorses of the FedEx fleet. I remember flying to Memphis to take a tour of the sprawling hub where a large percentage of packages and freight are removed from one plane, sorted by destination and put back on another. Going onboard a cavernous, empty MD-11 was unlike anything I had experienced—especially at 2 o'clock in the morning, which is when hub tours are given.

A couple of years later, I got another close-up look at an MD-11. I saw it in the wee hours too, but this one was upside down at Newark airport and in flames.

The phone in our bedroom rang at about 2:30 a.m. on July 31, 1997.

"Chris, this is Greg Rossiter at FedEx." Greg was second in command in the FedEx PR department. "A FedEx plane has crashed at Newark and it will be several hours before we can get there. I need you to go out there and assess the situation."

He gave me the details of where to go and who to ask for and I told him I would call him with a situation report. My next call was to Kiersten Zweibaum, my colleague on the FedEx account. We organized a car service, and off we went to Newark airport.

We could see the flames from the New Jersey Turnpike. We pulled up to the FedEx hanger and unchallenged by anyone, walked into the building and introduced ourselves. (This was before 9/11; security was a lot more lax than it is today.) In short order we found ourselves in a little bus heading out to the crash scene.

I am not sure what we were supposed to do out there. I sure as hell wasn't going to be able to spin this one away. And I wasn't going to be much help in putting out the fire. From the perimeter of the scene, I called Greg.

By then he had learned that there had been five people on board, and all had escaped with relatively minor injuries. Looking at the fire fighters and flames and upside-down FedEx logo, that seemed miraculous.

CNN began reporting that "eyewitnesses" had seen the plane explode in midair, which just never happened. What *had* happened is that the pilot, like many others apparently, got his jollies seeing how fast he could get a plane on the ground. That night, the plane came in too steeply and its tail struck the runway. The jet leaned to one side and the wing caught the tarmac, causing the plane to cart-wheel and land upside-down, pointing in the direction it had come from. Of course, we did not learn all of this until months later, when the National Transportation Safety Board issued its report.

In the meantime, Greg called to say that since no FedEx employee who was qualified to talk to the media could get to the scene, I was going to have to be the company spokesperson. CNN wanted someone on camera, the sooner the better. I was glad I had put on a suit.

PR people are supposed to stay behind the camera, not get in front of it. Greg fed me a statement, which I was able to memorize on the drive over to the balcony that CNN had commandeered, which looked right down on the wreckage.

It was daylight now, and the smoke was clearly visible behind me as the reporter, Gary Tuchman, introduced me as a FedEx spokesperson, which was technically a violation of ethics on my part. But I had come clean to him that I was a Ketchum employee, and he said that if I had been designated by FedEx to speak for the company, that was all he needed.

The camera lights came on. They were so bright and hot! Gary asked me what had happened, and I suddenly realized that my lips were moving and I was reciting the statement rather convincingly. But the whole time, there was a little voice in the back of my mind saying, "Oh God, don't let me fuck this up! Please God, don't let me fuck this up!"

At last the interview ended—it might have been all of 90 seconds, but it seemed like ten minutes. As the reporter made his closing remarks I sashayed off camera, relieved to be away from the hot lights in front of me and the flames behind me. The reporter called after me: "Just one thing. Next time we do this, stay next to me until I finish!" We were doing it again? In all, as the morning progressed, I ended up making three live appearances on CNN, plus some local broadcast outlets.

When I checked my voicemail, I must have had a dozen congratulatory calls from Ketchum colleagues all over the world who had seen the report. They said I had done a great job, but all I could think of was how glib I had been over the years as I instructed clients on how to deal with the media. I finally appreciated just how stressful a process it was, and resolved to be a little more empathetic in the future.

FedEx became a role model for issues management. We developed a comprehensive list of everything we could imagine going wrong (including a plane crash) and developed plans to try to keep something from happening or respond effectively if it did. An important component of this process was conducting a vulnerabilities assessment. We would get groups of executives together and blue-sky some of the things that kept them up at night.

Our team was dispatched to undertake such an exercise in Hong Kong, where the FedEx Asia-Pacific operations were headquartered. We gathered in a conference room where I went over to a whiteboard and wrote, "What potential crises keep you up at night?"

Immediately the president of the Asia-Pacific region raised his hand. "How about this? Consultant ruins expensive whiteboard by writing on it with a permanent marker?" *Aw, crap! Really?* In retrospect, if everybody who used that whiteboard for the next few years gave a moment's thought to what I had written, that wouldn't have been such a bad thing.

# # #

One day, I was summoned to a meeting with one of the agency's senior leaders, who asked if I would take over as the senior relationship manager for Dow Chemical, a Ketchum client. The person who had been in that role was moving on to something else and—fortuitously—the senior PR person at the company was brand new.

Dow had a practice of rotating line executives through the PR department for a year or two and then sending them back into operations roles. This would be a great time to make a switch at the top of our account team since Dow's new PR person had not formed a relationship with the agency person whose role I had been asked to take on.

I agreed to take on the new assignment, and made arrangements to travel to the firm's Midland, Michigan, headquarters to meet the new PR head, Sarah. The following week, I packed a bag and set out for the airport. The must-read book at the time was journalist Thomas Friedman's *The Lexus and the Olive Tree.* I was enjoying it very much and was looking forward to continuing to read it on the flight.

Sarah and I hit it off immediately. We spent the whole day together, and in the car on the way to lunch, I happened to mention how much I was enjoying my book. Sarah responded that she'd actually like to read it herself. I should have reached into my bag for the book and offered it to her on the spot. After all, I was in the client service business, and trying to bond with a new client! Instead, I held on to my copy, finished the book on the return flight, and when I got home, ordered the book for Sarah from Amazon.

Later in the week, I got a message on my voicemail that soon had me convulsed with laughter and no small degree of horror:

> Hi Chris, this is Louise, Sarah's assistant. We received a package today from Amazon. It looks like you were trying to send Sara a copy of *The Lexus and the Olive Tree*, but that's not what arrived. So call me and we'll straighten this out. And by the way, the book that did arrive is called *Ten Thousand Ways to Say I Love You!*...Have a nice weekend.

I called customer service at Amazon. As I explained what had occurred, the fellow in the call center started laughing so hard, I thought he was going to hurt himself. When he finally regained control, he apologized and offered to send a copy of the right book to Sarah—at no charge. And he said, with some amusement, that she could keep the other book too.

I am grateful that Sarah has a hearty sense of humor. We remained friends for years, and every now and then she would send an email with only a random four digit number in the body of the email: 5738 or 8637. Since I never got the book, I can't tell you which of the ten thousand ways those numbers referred to, but I always responded in kind. 3745, Sarah!

# # #

Once in a while (not often, thankfully), a client will throw the agency under the bus. When I got to Ketchum, the agency served the Entertainment, Media and Communications (EMC) group of Price Waterhouse. One day, the woman who was leading the EMC account for the agency came to my office. She looked stricken. I asked what was wrong and she told me an outrageous tale.

The head of the EMC group, a Price Waterhouse partner, had scored a big win—a big movie studio/production company. He directed his Ketchum team to put together a press release, and at his direction, the agency sent it out over the news wires.

That precipitated a call from someone at the upper reaches of another rather enormous Price Waterhouse client in the EMC space (think mouse ears). This person was not pleased that Price Waterhouse had taken an assignment from the competitor in the first place and, even worse, that the firm had made a big deal about it in the media. The partner back-pedaled furiously and told the client that it was all a surprise to him.

He then called the agency and demanded that *we* take responsibility for drafting and distributing the press release without his knowledge and without his permission. "But," our account leader protested, "that's not true and you know it. You directed us to issue that release. This is not our fault."

The partner replied: "I never said it was your fault. I said I am going to blame you."

This has got to be the most preposterous thing a client has ever said, and I'm not even sure what's in second place. (Well, probably, "If it's a big enough idea, we'll find the money.")

# # #

In 1999, the NYSE wanted to hire an agency to help it deal with the growing competitive threat from the Nasdaq, and Ketchum got the job. The dotcom craze was in its ascendancy, and the Nasdaq was viewed as the place for tech company IPOs.

Bob Zito was the NYSE's executive vice president of communications. He had spent a few years at Sony Music and learned a thing or two about show business. It was his idea to make the twice-daily ringing of the stock exchange's bell a media event. Until then, the bell-ringing had been carried out by a nondescript NYSE employee. Bob turned the trip to the bell podium into a celebrity event. Kings and heads of state, movie stars and professional athletes vied for the worldwide exposure brought by ringing the bell. Sarah Jessica Parker rang the bell on an episode of *Sex and the City*. The scene was filmed at night after the Exchange was closed, and the next week, Bob invited her to come and do it for real. "Oh my God!" she exclaimed. "It's exactly like we shot it!"

The tragic events of September 11 caused the Exchange to close for a week. Our team could not get anywhere near the Exchange's home at 11 Wall Street, but we were able to work the phones and invite reporters to NYSE press briefings in midtown. One of the most moving images I have ever seen was when members of the New York police and fire departments and the Port Authority police, along with a dozen politicians, crowded onto the balcony and rang the opening bell on September 17, reopening the US financial markets after their longest closure in history.

I was able to get down to the Exchange the next day, and the dust was so thick—even a full week after the attack—that I had to remove my contact lenses and throw them away. So many people at the Exchange had lost friends and loved ones that it was impossible to walk anywhere in the NYSE's offices and not see people wracked with tears.

One day in August 2003, two years after the attacks, Bob asked me to come down to the Exchange. He said they were going to issue a press release and he wanted to know what I thought. When I got there, he handed me a draft. The NYSE Board had voted to extend CEO Dick Grasso's contract. So far, so good. But further down in the release were these words:

> The NYSE distributed to Mr. Grasso his savings account balance of $40.0 million, his previously accrued retirement benefit of $51.6 million and his previously earned account balance of $47.9 million relating to prior incentive awards.

Now I understood why Bob wanted me to look at the release. While most people don't get their retirement funds until they actually retire, the NYSE board was giving Dick his at the same time they were offering him a new two-year contract. And the figures seemed astronomical, although to the Wall Street titans who sat on the board, $140 million must have seemed like chump change. But I knew—and Bob knew—that nothing good was going to come from this.

Sure enough, a firestorm erupted. Some media pundits were outraged that the head of a not-for-profit organization could be so lavishly compensated; others saw it as a just reward for terrific performance. CNBC reporter Charlie Gasparino was in the latter camp and was one of Dick's biggest supporters. He felt the furor over Dick's pay was nothing more than sour grapes.

I was a little perplexed. The naysayers were the same folks who barely whimpered when other CEOs made billions. But Dick was a polarizing figure within the Exchange and despite the board's apparent support, the continuing rage was being stoked, anonymously, by seat owners (people who paid six-figure sums for the right to trade on the floor of the Exchange) and, stunningly, individual board members.

Over the next few weeks, the controversy did not die down—it only got worse. In early September, I was forced to cut short a vacation in Canada and hightail it back to the Exchange as a growing chorus of calls for Dick's head grew louder.

On the morning of September 17, I was sitting with Bob Zito, Rob Flaherty and Dick in Dick's office. It was all-Dick-all-the-time on the flat screen on the wall. We discussed things we might do to quell the hysteria, but Dick waved his hand dismissively. "This will blow over in a couple of days," he said. That afternoon, the board asked for his resignation—two years to the day after Dick had been hailed for his crucial role in restarting the US capital markets after 9/11.

A board meeting was called at short notice; most of the board participated by phone. After Dick resigned, board member Carl McCall asked Bob Zito to put together a press release, but he needn't have bothered. By the time Bob went from Dick's sixth floor office to his own on the 12th floor, the story was already breaking on CNBC.

I have good reason to suspect that during the board meeting, the head of PR for one of the major investment banks whose chairman was a NYSE board member had his cell phone next to the speakerphone in the chairman's office—and two Wall Street Journal reporters were on the other end. According to another reporter who witnessed it, when Dick offered his resignation, the two reporters high-fived. Ugly stuff.

The following Sunday, I was again summoned to the Exchange for a telephone press conference in which John Reed, the former CEO of Citicorp, was named the Exchange's interim CEO. Reed wasn't in attendance, but he called in from the little island he owns off the coast of France. But the next week he was in place in Dick's former office.

One of the first things he did was to ask for the resignations of most of the board members. He then needed to identify new possible board members. Bob Zito and I were summoned to Reed's office. We found him sitting at the same conference table where Dick had sat the morning of the day he resigned.

Reed wanted to know if we thought he could get away with leaving former U.S. Secretary of State Madeleine Albright and BlackRock chairman Larry Fink on the board, since they were recent additions and had not had anything to do with the Grasso retirement affair. We told him we thought that would be okay. He then announced that his next move would be to diversify the board, asking if we had any suggestions.

At the time, my son was attending Rensselaer Polytechnic Institute in upstate New York, and the school's president was Shirley Ann Jackson, an African-American who, among other accomplishments, had led the Nuclear Regulatory Commission. I threw out her name.

Soon after, the Exchange announced that Dr. Jackson had agreed to join its board. Evidently, her very first contribution was to recommend to Reed that he get a new PR firm, somebody *good*. That's gratitude for you! I doubt that to this day, she has any idea that I was responsible for getting her the board seat in the first place.

#

Luckily, John Reed didn't listen to Dr. Jackson's advice and we continued to work for the Exchange. My wife and I have a dear friend who was head of human resources for a little electric utility in Vermont—Green Mountain Power. Small though it was, it was an NYSE-listed company.

My Ketchum team and I had actually written the policy governing who could ring the Exchange's opening bell, and it had to be someone spectacular. Subsidiaries of listed companies, non-profits and cause-related organizations could ring the closing bell at the Exchange's discretion, but not the opening bell. (Ironically, the opening bell is shown only on CNBC and CNN, but the closing bell is shown on all the U.S. networks' evening news programs and pretty much everywhere else worldwide. So from an exposure standpoint, the closing bell is actually the better deal.)

After I had talked big about writing the guidelines, our friend innocently asked if I could arrange a bell-ringing by Green Mountain. My sphincter tightened a few notches, and I said, "Sure, why not?" Served me right for talking big.

I went to Bob and he asked, "Who?" He looked up the company. "That is one small company, but they are listed. But I can't give you the opening bell—the president of Serbia has that sewn up. I suppose I could bounce the Girl Scouts for the closing bell ..."

I felt a twinge of guilt for bumping the Girl Scouts, but that was all I needed to hear. I locked it up and called our friend. She was elated. This turned out to be the biggest thing that had happened to Green Mountain Power since 110 volts! The company held a raffle, and 10 employees and spouses won plane tickets to New York to witness the event. The rest of the employees crowded around TVs at headquarters.

It was a Friday, and every Friday at the exchange is special. The exchange closes every day at 4 o'clock, but on Fridays at precisely 3:33:33 on the dot, the floor traders start making jungle noises—monkeys, elephants, birds—and by 3:34 the whole floor is overtaken with this bizarre cacophony. I hadn't warned our friend or her fellow employees about this ritual, which I had heard about but never actually experienced. We were all shocked and delighted.

Finally, the CEO of Green Mountain Power came out onto the bell podium and at precisely 4 o'clock, to thunderous applause, pressed the button to ring the bell and close the exchange. Our friend was a hero at Green Mountain Power, I was a hero to our friend, and Bob was a hero to me.

Bob's departure marked the end of the NYSE-Ketchum relationship, and about that time, I got a call from my former Burson pal Al Tortorella. He was the head of the corporate practice at Ogilvy Public Relations and he wanted to know if I would have lunch with him. By then, without realizing it I had somehow become a "Ketchum person." I had been made a partner, and was in charge of the global corporate practice. I had great accounts and worked with the best teams ever. I loved the place. It was family. I had no intention of going anywhere else.

But it would be nice to have lunch with Al. "Sure, " I said. "Why not?"

# # #

MY OGILVY COLLEAGUE AL TORTORELLA was considered by many to be the dean of crisis counselors; his resume included (while at Burson-Marsteller) the infamous Tylenol poisoning incident; the disaster at the Union Carbide Bhopal, India, plant; and the worldwide Perrier recall. Al had been enticed to Ogilvy Public Relations to lead its global corporate practice. But after a year or two, Al found the prospect of managing a large group less and less interesting. He ached for a good old industrial spill or a corporate scandal rather than a spreadsheet.

Al invited me to lunch along with Paul Hicks, who was the US CEO of Ogilvy PR, which is to say the entire firm. (Many years earlier, the US firm had separated from the rest of the global network, and while still a subsidiary of Ogilvy & Mather, the massive advertising agency, it was run separately from the rest of Ogilvy PR.) During lunch, I let Al and Paul know that I didn't see a move in the future.

But then began a campaign that lasted for several months: drinks, breakfasts with other senior Ogilvy people, dinner with the chairman and, notably, the promise of oodles and oodles of money. Eventually, they wore me down, and with a great deal of ambivalence, I accepted the position of managing director of the global corporate practice at Ogilvy Public Relations. I didn't realize I was about to step into my own crisis.

The "global" part of my title was ironic since Ogilvy PR only did business in the US. But soon that changed. Not long after I got to Ogilvy, the chairman, Marcia Silverman, and Paul Hicks convened a meeting of the firm's management committee. Ogilvy PR was rejoining the Ogilvy & Mather mothership and once again, we would be managed as a global agency.

Most important, we would now have unfettered access to O&M's prestigious advertising client base for possible PR work. In theory, that was very appealing, but in reality, advertising people don't really understand PR or PR people, and we had to spend a lot of time explaining to the advertising folks why bringing in the PR team to supplement the advertising campaign was a win-win.

Under orders by O&M leadership, advertising creative directors and account teams tried to work a PR program into their pitches, but clearly, enthusiasm was lacking. We PR people were supposedly given 30 minutes at the end of each 90-minute advertising pitch to present our PR ideas. Naturally, the ad pitch always ran long and the PR team would have 68 seconds to present the result of weeks of labor—usually while the clients and our own advertising colleagues were gathering their things and preparing to leave.

It was maddening.

# # #

Of course, not every intersection with the ad folks was dispiriting. An exception was the German-owned overnight delivery service DHL, which was mounting an all-out assault on FedEx and UPS. DHL had a strong presence in Europe and Asia, but had not enjoyed much success in the U.S., despite having been founded in California in the early 1970s.

The creative team at Ogilvy advertising welcomed the PR team and it was a great collaboration. The advertising was funny and well executed, with a number of promotional and public relations tie-ins. It really was a textbook example of how several marketing disciplines can work together to create something powerful and effective.

And that, of course, was the problem.

While the Ogilvy teams were working at peak efficiency, DHL had neglected to prepare for the amazing success of the ads and PR tactics. Literally overnight, demand for DHL services by frustrated FedEx or UPS customers skyrocketed. And DHL was completely unprepared for the onslaught of packages and envelopes flooding in.

Within a couple of weeks, horror stories of lost or damaged packages became commonplace, and within a month, many (if not most) of the new DHL customers were returning to FedEx and UPS. The client pulled the advertising and PR efforts.

The Ogilvy creative director best summed it up: "It was a case of great advertising and PR making a promise the client couldn't deliver on."

# # #

On the other side of the spectrum was the joint pitch for Ameriprise Financial, which had recently been spun off from American Express. The advertising creative team was completely uninterested in working with the PR team. Meanwhile, the creative director had become obsessed with the idea of installing soothing quiet zones in airports, where travelers could relax between flights.

Each of these quiet zones would be outfitted with specially designed lounge chairs. The chairs were enormous, and shaped rather like half of an eggshell split lengthwise. Once engulfed by one of these artificial wombs, travelers would be lulled by the sounds of an Ameriprise commercial.

Ameriprise had recently moved into a building in the financial district, and while most of the office space gleamed, the conference room our pitch was going to be in was on a floor that was still under renovation.

The conference room itself was nice enough but just outside the door, the carpet had not been installed and there were large holes in the sheetrock walls along the hallway.

The creative director had rented one of the eggshell chairs and somehow convinced the building management to allow him to install it at the client site. It took several hours to truck the behemoth to the loading dock and get it positioned on the floor where we were presenting. But when I walked into the conference room, I didn't see it and I know I would have because it was huge, white and weighed a ton.

The clients arrived and we launched into our pitch. As usual, the advertising team ran over, and our PR team delivered a whole campaign plan in about a minute and a half. The clients thanked us and rose to leave, when the creative director sprang from his seat and said, "Before you go, we have something to show you."

One of the clients looked at his watch and said he was sorry but he had another meeting. Several others agreed and suddenly we were alone. The creative director was stunned. "Please, it will just take a moment...please!" he called to the backs of the retreating clients. We followed him as he walked out of the room, down the semi-darkened hallway and into a room with a concrete floor and metal studs in view. There was the chair, forlorn and looking small in the cavernous space. The creative director, looking depressed and on the verge of tears, settled into the lounge chair and closed his eyes. That was the last I ever saw of him.

# # #

One day, I got a call from the guy in charge of the Tokyo office. He asked if I would be able to travel to Japan to give an overview of investor relations in the U.S. to a group of Japanese executives. I checked in with my boss, Ogilvy PR chairman Marcia Silverman, suggesting that while I was over there, I should drop in on the Hong Kong, Shanghai and Beijing offices. She agreed and I booked my trip. I was excited because although I had been to Hong Kong many times and Tokyo once before, I had never been to either Shanghai or Beijing.

Once my presentation was finished, I then I flew on to Hong Kong and as I walked off the plane on Friday night, my Blackberry started chirping. There was a message from a very senior guy at Ogilvy & Mather in New York. The subject line was "Urgent Message!" And there were three or four of them.

Evidently, O&M had won the Lenovo PC account—Lenovo had purchased IBM's ThinkPad business—and there was going to be a major summit meeting the following Friday. I explained my predicament: I was in Asia and not planning to be back until the Monday following the big meeting.

We started communicating in real time—it was 9 p.m. in Hong Kong and 9 a.m. in New York. He said that it was absolutely vital that I attend this meeting. I shot a note off to Marcia, asking for guidance. She said she guessed I didn't have much choice. So I told the O&M guy I would be there.

I flew back to Tokyo and eventually boarded a nonstop flight to New York. As soon as the plane touched down, I turned on my Blackberry. There was a message just an hour old from the O&M guy: "Meeting Canceled."

And I have still never been to Beijing or Shanghai.

When I got a call from the Korn Ferry executive search firm, asking if I might be interested in something else, my response was, "Sure, why not?"

Interlude:
Maybe It Really Is Rocket Science

Over the years I have written and spoken a great deal about crisis preparedness and response. One point I often stress is that the best way to manage a crisis is not to have one in the first place, and this is why doing a regular vulnerabilities assessment is the key component of issues management.

Such an assessment usually entails a structured process that identifies internal and external problems that, if left unattended, could explode into a crisis—maybe not tomorrow, but perhaps next month or next year. The whole point of issues management is to know what could happen and take preemptive action to avoid having to launch a full-blown crisis response.

The rudiments of issues management are simple enough. Start with *identification*. What kinds of unpleasant things might happen to your company? Answers can range from operational issues (accidents, product defects, denial-of-service hacking and other cyberattacks) to longer-term issues (legislative or regulatory initiatives, labor relations or HR issues). A perusal of a week's worth of *The Wall Street Journal* will yield plenty of instances of acts of God and vagaries of man, which will inspire and possibly depress you.

Next, *prioritization.* What is the likelihood that a given issue will grow in severity and what would the impact be on your company if it did? An asteroid colliding with Earth would ruin pretty much everybody's day, but I wouldn't spend a minute thinking about how I might prevent that from happening. But I wonder if executives at music companies might have changed course 10 years ago if they had stopped to ponder the then-unthinkable revolution in music consumption and gotten ahead of it early.

The last step: *monitoring and influencing.* This is the act of putting issues management into motion. By following current developments for a particular issue, you can plan and implement steps to alter its course or inoculate your company against it.

An issues-management assessment can be very sophisticated (and very expensive), or it can be sketched out on an envelope. What's important is that you take the time to blue-sky the issues that could realistically become big problems in the future and consider how you might forestall that outcome. Unfortunately, squeezing in the time to do these assessments is hard. Find the time.

And be mindful of the words of aerospace engineer Ed Murphy. He passed away in 1990, but his most notable contribution to the world remains as relevant as ever. After graduating from West Point, Ed served in the Army Air Corps during World War II. When the war ended, he enrolled in the Air Force Institute of Technology, and in due course became a rocket scientist. Ed's job was to design and perfect safety and life support systems for NASA—it's no exaggeration to say that lives depended on his work, which he took very seriously. He approached each new system, designed by engineers who assumed that their creation would work, with the assumption that it would fail. His job was to figure out why and how to prevent such a failure. He coined the adage, "Anything that can go wrong, will." Today we know his saying as Murphy's Law—an excellent credo for PR professionals dealing with crisis management.

Chapter Seven

The View from the Other
Side of the Fence

AFTER 26 YEARS IN THE agency business, I had always thought it would be a good idea to experience life on the other side of the fence, the company side. (This is a thought that should come to you after about 10 years into your career, but back then I was having too much fun.)

When things started looking grim at Ogilvy, I put out some feelers and went on a few interviews in pursuit of a corporate job, but my lack of prior experience on the client side was a big disadvantage. I wasn't sure why (although I am now). I thought that my extended on-site experience at FedEx and the NYSE had given me a sense of life in a corporate environment—at the NYSE, I had my own office next to Bob Zito.

Now, with the best part of a decade in the corporate world under my belt, I can see just how different the experience is. For one thing, as a consultant, if your advice doesn't work out, you can move on to another client. But as an employee, if you recommend something and it doesn't pan out, you will live with that stain forever.

When Korn Ferry called, I thought I was just the right guy for the position they were proposing. The job was vice president of communications at Standard & Poor's, the credit rating agency. I was intrigued—I really did not understand what a credit rating agency was or what it did. It turns out that hardly anybody else did either. But a big focus of my career had been the financial markets and I was sure I could learn what I needed to quickly.

I joined Standard & Poor's in the spring of 2006, and all was quiet when I got there. The financial markets were soaring and S&P's business was keeping pace. There were no significant issues facing the company, and I was able to spend the first year establishing myself and learning about the company.

S&P had a number of businesses. Credit ratings were dominant, but there was also a very impressive index business, known throughout the world for its Standard & Poor's 500 index—a key indicator of stock market (if not economic) health. (A side note about the S&P 500: Not a day passed without a reporter asking, "How many stocks are in the S&P 500?") There was also an equities research business that had languished over the years. The ratings and indices were the real growth opportunities.

The first thing I had to learn was just what a credit rating was. At its simplest, a credit rating is an opinion about the likelihood that the principal and interest of an obligation (usually a bond) will be paid in full and on time. The stronger the likelihood, the higher the rating. The highest rating of all is AAA, and by the time I got to S&P, only five companies merited a triple A. In fact, most corporate debt was (and still is) rated below BBB-, meaning it was considered "junk." Which means that there is a higher likelihood that thus rated companies will default on their debt than triple A rated companies.

Bond ratings are given to companies, countries, states and municipalities, and over the years, these ratings have proven to be reliable indicators of creditworthiness. But bond ratings are also used in structured finance, and that is where all the trouble lay during my time at S&P.

Structured finance is not as complicated as you might think. Any cash flow can be securitized. Wait…that sounds complicated, doesn't it? Here's an example: Student loans have a predictable cash flow created by the monthly payments you or your child make each month. An investment bank might buy up a few thousand of these student loans that together earn an average interest rate of 6 percent. The bank takes the whole portfolio of loans and cuts it into slices that pay investors something less than 6 percent. Each of these slices has its own credit rating. The slice with the least risk might be assigned a rating of "AA+" but would pay a lower interest rate—maybe 2 percent. The "A" rated slice will pay a slightly higher interest rate because it has a slightly higher risk of default. And a "BBB" rated slice will pay a still higher interest rate but has a much higher risk of default. An investor will buy one of these securities according to his or her needs for investment returns and appetite for risk. Got it?

Student loans are far from the only loans that are securitized: car loans, industrial equipment loans and credit card debt all find their way into structured securities. And in the mid-2000s, the hottest structured securities of all were residential mortgage-backed securities, known as RMBS. I think you can see where this is leading.

RMBS became extremely popular because they accomplished many interesting things at once. They tended to pay better than average returns. And because most people pay their mortgages before anything else, RMBS had a reputation for being one of the least risky investments. Finally, the existence of RMBS meant that local bankers, whose capital would otherwise have been tied up in mortgages, could sell those loans at a profit to a securitizer, enabling them to fund even more mortgage loans.

RMBS had been around for a long time, and their default rates were as predictable as the movement of the sun. But as we were to learn, there was a dark side to RMBS. Because they were so much in demand as investments, securitizers could not create enough of them. They gave incentives to bankers to issue more mortgages, which fueled an explosion in what had been a sleepy business: mortgage brokers.

Mortgage brokers work with banks and other funding companies on a fee basis. The more mortgages they can produce, the more money they make. What happened during the subprime crisis of 2007–2009 was that mortgage brokers encouraged prospective buyers to buy the biggest possible house they could. The brokers had no reason to care how the loans would later perform, and thus no concern for the borrower's ability to make the monthly payments. Mortgage brokers would suggest that borrowers obtain an interest-only mortgage and then flip the house several months later for a big profit. These loans were considered "subprime" and they would be bundled together as "subprime RMBS."

This actually worked—until it stopped working. Subprime borrowers often used their homes like ATMs, taking out second and even third mortgages to buy electronics, vacations, anything at all. After a few months (in the hottest markets) they could sell their homes for double the original purchase price, settle up their debts and do it all over again.

But by 2008, the housing market began to cool off. Normally, when one geographic market slows down, it is offset by gains in markets that are still growing. So securitizers mixed up their portfolios to provide a sensible degree of geographic diversity.

Credit ratings on RMBS were predicated in some measure on this geographic diversity. But what if the housing market were to collapse everywhere at once? "Inconceivable!" said everyone in the securitization daisy chain. But that is exactly what happened.

For the first time, we began to see a steep rise in what were called first payment defaults. This is what happens when the home buyer can't afford to make the first payment on the mortgage when it comes due. And since the home buyer owed more than the house was worth, flipping was out of the question. The only option was to mail the keys to the lender and walk away. (Bankers called it "jingle mail.") Since it turned out that a lot of these homes were purchased as investments, it wasn't even painful for the buyer to default. And long past the point when the downturn must have been obvious to real estate professionals, they kept pushing less and less qualified buyers into more and more ridiculously priced homes.

All during the spring of 2007, there was a lot of head-scratching and frowning in the S&P's structured finance department. And then on July 10, we issued a press release that pretty much popped the bubble: S&P placed $6 billion in subprime RMBS on Credit-Watch Negative, indicating an imminent downgrade in the ratings. We specifically cited fraud and misrepresentation in the underwriting process. And with that move, we were off to the races.

The figure of $6 billion sounds a little quaint now. By the time the crisis was over, we were downgrading highly rated securities at $500 billion a clip. I was on the other end of the phone with reporters every time we did this. Especially in the beginning, I would get calls from real estate reporters who were so intimidated by our explanations that they would frequently blurt, "I don't care about all that, it's financial gobbledygook. Just tell me who's going to get hurt by your company." I generally declined. But they had a point.

It was sometimes a little mind-bending to consider the ingenious ways Wall Street found to separate investors from their money. Apart from RMBS, there were collateralized debt obligations, or CDOs, which bundled hundreds of RMBS into a single security. Then there was the CDO^2 and the synthetic CDO, which was no different than putting all of your chips on red at a roulette wheel. The whole thing reminded me of nothing so much as the line from Upton Sinclair's novel *The Jungle*, when one of the characters in a slaughterhouse brags, "They use everything of the pig but the squeal."

As you probably know, the collapse of the RMBS market in the United States eventually infected capital markets around the world, and the country was plunged into recession. RMBS were certainly not the sole cause, but they became the most visible. The three rating agencies that had been responsible for rating most of the problematic securities took the lion's share of the blame.

The most frequent rating-agency criticism was of the business model, in which securities issuers paid the ratings firms for their ratings. But that criticism seems off base to me. We pay doctors for their services and assume they're telling us the truth. Yet somehow a rating agency accepting a fee for its analysis of a security is corrupt.

Unlike doctors, S&P publishes its rating methodology on its website, so anyone can see exactly what assumptions and factors are used in formulating the rating of any security. (In fact, many savvy investors did just that and were able to figure out in advance what we were going to do. They made billions.)

S&P also publishes all its ratings and methodologies for free, which dramatically improves transparency in the markets. In the early days of credit ratings, investors paid for the ratings and did so precisely to get a leg up on investors who did not have that information.

Suffice it to say that my four years at S&P were the longest and most intense of my career. Still, there are moments I can look back on and chuckle. Once I got a call from Charlie Gasparino, the CNBC guy who had defended Dick Grasso so staunchly.

"Hey, it's Charlie," he said. "I've got one question: Are you guys stupid or greedy?"

"Can't we be both?" I responded.

That elicited a laugh, but he still trounced us on the air that day. Talking about how mentally and morally challenged the rating agencies were became a can-you-top-this contest. Every day brought a new punch in the gut. A deposition had turned up an instant message sent late one night by a young, very tired analyst to a colleague. It read: "A cow could structure a security and we'd rate it." She was, of course, being sarcastic. I dug into this and as far as I know, S&P never rated any securities structured by cows, sheep or any other livestock.

In another interesting twist, I had first learned about RMBS in the 1980s from reading Michael Lewis' great book, *Liar's Poker*, in which he chronicles his early career at Salomon Brothers. When he called us to ask about meeting with some of the structured finance people, we welcomed him and spent quite a while chatting about his recent bestseller, *Moneyball*, which was being made into a movie. Lewis was charming and informed, but he ripped us a new one in his next book, *The Big Short*, portraying the rating agencies as rubes who were not up to their task.

I did have the chance to pull a rabbit out of my hat from time to time. S&P's president gave an interview to Bloomberg News in which he misspoke. And I'm not talking about confusing "which" and "that." It was a mistake that was bound to become Exhibit A in the litigation we knew was coming.

I was able to convince the editor that it was a harmless mistake and he agreed to take the quote out. The story ran and all was well in the kingdom. But Bloomberg also publishes some of its content in a monthly magazine, and somehow the offending quote got left in. I got an advance copy and was apoplectic. I called the editor and to his credit, he ran right to the managing editor and in what was probably the most painful financial decision they made that year, they destroyed the entire print run of the magazine, which was sitting on a loading dock in London awaiting shipping. The article was edited and the magazine went back on press. I didn't try to get any stories there for a while.

Our general counsel told me that if that story had run as it was, it could have cost the company tens of millions or more in litigation. Alas, even though I like to think that I saved the company millions of bucks, none of it ever found its way into my bonus.

# # #

Not every sticky situation I lived through at S&P was related to mortgage securities. One kerfuffle involved a coffee shop in Dallas, Texas.

The owner of the shop had named her establishment Standard & Pours, and she had given her various concoctions names like "S&P 500 blend." Unfortunately, our lawyers felt that her business was infringing the Standard & Poor's trademark. This may seem trivial, but unfortunately, if you allow someone to infringe, you can actually lose your right to the trademark. That's why you'll see companies like Johnson & Johnson and Kimberly Clark emphasize that "Band-Aid" and "Kleenex" are brands, even though people use the names generically.

Our lawyers contacted the owner and asked her to stop using the Standard & Pours name. Immediately, her loyal customers sprang into action, and before long, I was fielding media calls from Dallas and around the country, asking why we, a giant corporation, were kicking the little guy. It was one of the rare instances where friends of mine actually took notice of S&P and wondered why we were being so hard-assed.

The owner was interviewed on national TV. I had been tipped to the segment in advance by the legal blogger at *The Wall Street Journal*, who was also going to be interviewed and wanted to know the facts.

Sadly for the owner, nobody had given her any media training and her interview was somewhat incoherent. The WSJ blogger was much better prepared and made the case that we had no choice but to take the actions we did. In the end, the owner realized that she had no choice.

Soon thereafter, she changed the name of the shop to Opening Bell Coffee. CNBC owns the trademark for Opening Bell, so she was their problem after that.

# # #

Throughout all of the stress and strain that accompanied those days, I am especially pleased to say that the members of my team never gave up, never let our critics' relentless sniping and finger-pointing slow them down. Many of them are still there. One person who did not stay was the head of communications, Marjory Appel. When a company is down for the count, the communications person always takes a hit, as if he or she had created the problem. I'm glad that Marjory later became the global communications leader at a major law firm.

Elizabeth Ventura, late of the late Bear Stearns, was hired and we hit it off immediately. But she is a hard-core basketball fan, and just a few months after she started, she left to become the head of PR for the NBA. Many feel it's one of the top ten jobs in all of PR. In her short tenure, Elizabeth fought hard for her team, and when she left, we felt a little abandoned.

Catherine Mathis, formerly with The New York Times, came on board as the new senior vice president. By 2011, things were quieting down, with the markets starting to recover. McGraw-Hill, S&P's benevolent owner, decided to split up the firm—credit ratings in one division and the rest in another. For those of us who had had S&P-wide responsibilities (including the president, Catherine and me), it was a bit of a demotion. As I was reworking the organization chart (some of my people now reported elsewhere), I said to my wife, "You know, the only job on this chart that doesn't really make sense is…mine."

The phone had basically stopped ringing, and ironically I kind of missed the action. I had made a lot of friends in the media, but most had moved on to other beats and had lost interest in S&P. I'd been with the firm for five years, and just when I was beginning to think it might be time to move on, an agency friend called to ask if I would have any interest in the head PR job at PricewaterhouseCoopers.

"Sure," I said. "Why not?"

# # #

My first experience with accounting firms came when I was at Hill and Knowlton. We had been selected by the firm then known as Deloitte Haskins & Sells, one of the Big Eight accounting firms. The Big Eight were ahead of the rest of the professional services firms in embracing marketing. Over the years, I have had many of the Big Eight as clients at one agency or another. We had Peat Marwick at Burson for a while, and then we served Anderson Consulting (now Accenture) as it acrimoniously broke away from the Arthur Anderson mothership. And, of course, Price Waterhouse had been a client at Ketchum.

In the late 1990s, Price Waterhouse merged with Coopers & Lybrand. The result was a mouthful: PricewaterhouseCoopers, or PwC. Some of the people I had worked with in my Ketchum days were still there, although thankfully, not the odious cretin who years earlier had told the Ketchum team, "I never said it was your fault. I said I am going to blame you." He had slithered on to another firm.

After having endured the financial crisis at S&P, I was looking forward to starting at a firm that had emerged relatively unscathed. I was in charge of public relations and internal communications, and had my work cut out for me because the teams I inherited— some 40 professionals—had been without any real leadership for 18 months. They were feeling a little unloved and their morale was in the cellar.

But what great teams they were! Many had been with the firm for more than a dozen years and their skill and knowledge of the firm made my job a lot easier. For reasons that elude me even today, the internal and external communications teams had never worked together—in some cases, the PR person for a given practice area had never met the internal communications person for the same area.

The first thing I did was get the leadership of the PR and internal communications teams boozed up and well fed at a nearby steakhouse. Food is love. We spent the next day in a conference room at the Harvard Club discussing ways to work together and share information. I began to see a glimmer of optimism in their eyes.

Before long, the teams were collaborating and producing results that started getting noticed by the firm's leadership. Partners who had stopped calling on PR and internal communications for support started calling again. In fact, we were soon oversubscribed and the firm responded generously: I was allowed to hire eight new professionals. That was something of a feat, since it was the partners' money I was spending.

One of the peculiarities of PwC is that it is highly mobile and decentralized. More than half of my teams worked from home or in other offices than New York. I was used to managing a team I could see. I had to get used to the idea that I would never get them all in one room at the same time. Fortunately, this was a group of self-starters who knew when to ask for help but enjoyed not having the boss looking over their shoulder all the time. And there was always something happening that demanded my attention elsewhere.

# # #

During the run-up to the 2012 presidential election, a big campaign issue was whether and when Mitt Romney would release his tax returns. Traditional and social media were salivating to see what secrets Romney's returns would reveal, but for whatever reason, the Romney campaign was hesitating to release them. PwC had prepared Romney's returns for many years—that was a matter of public record since the firm's name appears at the bottom. But we referred all media calls to the campaign. Our policy was never to discuss clients or our work for them.

One morning, I received a call that changed that. A man in Tennessee was claiming that he had somehow broken into the PwC office in Nashville and downloaded Romney's tax returns. He demanded $1 million (to be paid in Bitcoin) for their return or he would release them to the media. As his bona fides, he sent an encrypted flashdrive to the local media. They couldn't read the files, but they could not say for sure that they were not genuine.

Not surprisingly, social media grabbed this story and ran with it. I started getting calls from our monitoring folks telling me that Twitter was blowing up about the alleged break. I knew that we needed to respond quickly, so I wrote a tweet: "At this time, there is no evidence that our systems have been compromised and we are working with the Secret Service." That's it, 117 characters. I sent it off to the general counsel and the leadership team for approval.

Although the general counsel was fine with it, one of the leadership team members was uncomfortable. "What if it turns out that it really happened?" he asked. I knew that the firm tracked virtually every keystroke of every employee. It was only possible to download data onto a PwC-encrypted flash drive, so the system obviously tracked when someone used or tried to use an unapproved drive. And the identity of anyone accessing sensitive data like tax returns and audit materials was tracked. Nevertheless, in the unbelievably small likelihood that a breach had occurred, I thought we were covered.

"See that part that says, 'At this time?'" I asked. "Is it true that *at this time* we have no such evidence?"

"But what if later it turns out to be true? We'll look ridiculous," the partner said.

"No more ridiculous than if we spend another ten minutes not responding." The group voted and approved the tweet.

Within 15 minutes of my tweeting the statement, the hysteria started dying down and the volume of tweets began descending as people absorbed the ridiculousness of the ransom demand (few people had even heard of Bitcoin back then) and by day's end, the media calls had dried up. Too bad it took three hours to get approval of that tweet.

It turned out that the alleged data-napper was a serial offender and had attempted a similar extortion of an insurance company a few years earlier. Although the Secret Service was never able to fully break the encryption of the flash drive, they did find a photograph of the man's cat on it. First rule of extortion: Use a new flash drive.

# # #

During my time at PwC, I discovered that I could still be surprised by the behavior of some reporters. (I had thought my days at S&P would have inured me.)

PwC was one of the largest employers in Tampa, Florida, because it is where our back office operations were based. From time to time, the firm needed to relocate within the city to larger quarters to accommodate additional employees. You might think that would be considered a good thing for Tampa; the local Tampa government thought so and repeatedly offered the firm financial incentives to keep our operations in the city. But the local media were incensed that we would even consider accepting such largesse. They had an almost irrational dislike for the firm and were always on the hunt for some dirt about PwC.

Not too long after I joined the firm, someone—it was not immediately clear who—had committed suicide in the large atrium in the center of our building in Tampa, jumping from a fourth floor balcony to the lobby floor. It turned out that it had been an employee of the company that managed the vending machines in the pantries, but the police asked us to keep that confidential until the family of the deceased was notified. We could, however, confirm that it was not a PwC employee if asked.

Sure enough, we got a call from the local paper. "I hear you've had an incident," the reporter announced.

My media relations person handling the calls responded, "Yes, there has been a tragic incident. I can tell you that it was not a PwC employee."

The reporter replied, "Oh really? Then I'm not interested." And he hung up.

He would only have been interested in telling a story that painted PwC as a firm whose employees were so unhappy, they were throwing themselves to certain death. You don't come across that kind of cynicism every day.

Interlude:
The 60-Minute Challenge

Just how much can you get done in 60 minutes?

If your organization became the center of a crisis, in 60 minutes could you:

- Get management and legal to approve a statement and post it on Twitter, Facebook, LinkedIn and the corporate website?

- Shoot and upload a video of the CEO responding to the crisis?

- Brief vital external constituents, such as regulators and legislators?

- Record a blast voicemail message informing all employees of the incident and reminding them to refer external inquiries, especially media, to corporate communications?

- Monitor social media traffic and the evolution of the story?

- Do all of this while fielding an onslaught of media, customer, legislator and employee calls and emails?

It wasn't so long ago that fielding a response to a crisis within eight hours was considered good, and four hours was miraculous, especially given the time needed for internal legal, management and regulatory review.

In the third quarter of 2012, the world reached a milestone. More than 1 billion smartphones were in use globally. One billion people are now armed with the technology to photograph, video, tweet, post or otherwise report on your organization—and it's rarely good news. In not much more time than it took me to type this sentence, your company's supposed failings can be tweeted, retweeted, YouTubed, Facebooked, LinkedIn-ed, remixed and re-blogged. All of a sudden, one little post or tweet has become a very big problem.

Fueled by technology and social media, pressure on communicators has accelerated to the point where today you've got about an hour—one hour!—to respond to fast-moving events. That's the standard. This surely accounts for why numerous studies have shown public relations to be second only to air traffic controller as the most stressful occupation. And among PR people, crisis communications specialists have it the worst.

Just how much can you get done in an hour? If you haven't thought about this by the time a crisis hits, then the answer is probably: not much. Long before Armageddon knocks on your door, you need to answer the six questions listed above. And that's just for starters. Time spent thinking about how to mobilize the people necessary to achieve the 60-minute response—and gaining their commitment to do it—is worth 100 times what you put into it. But even then, you'll only have a schematic for the machine, not the raw ingredients to make it churn.

Assembling those ingredients—approved statements, tweets, Facebook posts, video and the like—eats up precious minutes. And the technology we have at our disposal today often means we can make bigger mistakes faster than ever. Tweeting the wrong thing can worsen the situation. Organizations that take risk-management seriously anticipate crises and are prepared with high-level response plans. The all-important difference between a "problem" and a "crisis" is the moment your customers and other stakeholders are hearing about the issue through every possible channel—except yours.

Most of the time, we know what people need to hear: that the company is concerned about the problem and is committed to finding and reporting the facts as soon as possible. Simply tweeting those sentiments can slow down the re-tweets and the digital piling-on, allowing you the chance to engage in a more constructive dialogue. The key is communicating through every available channel as effectively and as quickly as you can. And that takes forethought.

Talk to management *now* about the need to respond fast—in what may seem to them to be breathtaking speed. Try out the content of the early responses you'd be prepared to issue. Today most management teams understand the importance of risk management and the need to respond effectively and quickly to a crisis.

You might start by posing this question: "If a crisis were to occur, how would we want our company to be seen by our most important constituents a year later?" If the answer is "A valued asset in our community, well-managed and competent in a tough situation," then there is no substitute for foresight and preparation. That includes getting the CEO to agree that at a moment's notice he or she will need to drop everything and sit down in front of a camera, and also identifying an appropriate stand-in if the CEO is not available.

When the crisis hits, you'll have to work fast to tailor your response to the specific situation. Preparing your tools in advance and gaining a commitment to speedy engagement from the top will greatly shorten the time it takes to mount an effective response.

Are you prepared to be a "60 minute" responder? Getting this right is one of the most important contributions we can make to our companies.

Final Thoughts

ONE OF THE CURIOUS THINGS about the PR business is how hard it is to explain exactly what it is, other than to say, "PR is what PR people do." If I were an academic, I suppose I might say: "Public relations is the methodology and practice of a comprehensive, interrelated spectrum of strategies, tools and tactics frequently employed in the provision of public relations services by public relations practitioners." There, that clears things up!

I doubt that there is anyone in the business who has not had the conversation that goes something like this:

> Aunt Sophie: So tell me, dear, what is it you do for a living?
>
> PR Person: Public relations.
>
> Aunt Sophie: Come again? What's that?
>
> PR Person: We try to get stories about our clients into newspapers, magazines and online publications.
>
> Aunt Sophie: So it's like advertising.

PR Person, with a sigh: Yeah, just like advertising.

Aunt Sophie: Mort! Mort! I told you, she's in advertising, just like on "Mad Men." How exciting. How naughty!

PR Person: *Sigh.*

I suspect that the astonishing number of disciplines that fall under the "public relations" umbrella will forever stymie attempts to pin down a definition. Not too long ago, the Public Relations Society of America (PRSA) labored mightily to come up with a definition of PR that neither excluded nor pissed off anyone: "Public relations is a strategic communication process that builds mutually beneficial relationships between organizations and their publics." With all due respect to PRSA, to me that doesn't seem much better than "PR is what PR people do."

Then again, a more precise definition might do the business more harm than good. The amorphous nature of PR has allowed its practitioners to embrace an ever-growing panoply of communications tools and tactics.

The job may entail calling a reporter to pitch a story; presenting to physicians at a medical convention; dressing up as a pickle and getting on the "Today" show; dropping a 10-foot tortilla chip into a giant bowl of salsa; developing LinkedIn profiles for busy executives; or providing strategic advice to a beleaguered board of directors. And no matter which of these activities you undertake, you can still tell Aunt Sophie that you're in PR.

The diversity of offerings under the heading of PR and the fact that so many PR programs are custom tailored to fit a client's particular circumstances make it particularly hard to capture the essence of PR. That's why most academic books on public relations rely so heavily on case studies of successful PR campaigns. Rather than instruct students in how to do something, these case studies illustrate how somebody else did something in hopes that the reader can transfer that knowledge to a different situation. There is nothing inherently wrong with that approach, but it is a primary reason that efforts to professionalize the business have proven so hard.

The PR practitioner's ongoing lament is that CEOs and senior management of major corporations do not take the business more seriously. It is hard to imagine a CEO not giving serious thought to her company's PR and reputation when something bad happens. But a large percentage of the work of the PR department does not need a CEO's attention. Few senior executives I know pour over the details of a media plan for a trade show.

Every now and then, a senior PR leader calls for some kind of official certification for PR practitioners. Good luck with that. But the idea is not entirely without merit.

It is interesting to me that you need a license to cut hair in all 50 U.S. states, but there is no licensing requirement to practice PR anywhere in the country. Yet if you botch someone's coif, the problem fixes itself (in time). Screw up somebody's reputation and the stain can last forever.

Being licensed doesn't guarantee that you are any good at what you do. We read about too many wayward doctors, lawyers and accountants to believe that. But it does mean that a practitioner has met specific educational requirements and demonstrated some minimal level of competency to the licensing authority. By conferring a license, the authority reserves the right to take it away if it determines that the practitioner is incompetent and has caused harm. And the penalties for practicing without a license can be quite severe.

Many licensed professionals are required to seek continuing education units to help them stay up to date on the latest developments in their field or to learn new methods and tactics.

The closest the PR business gets to any kind of certification is voluntary accreditation by the PRSA. According to the Bureau of Labor Statistics, there are some 250,000 practitioners in the U.S., and only a small fraction pursue accreditation.

It doesn't seem likely that there is ever going to be a requirement to have a license to practice PR, nor that such a requirement would result in a substantive improvement in the quality of the work we PR people do. And that's too bad because increasingly I find that some areas of our business could use a little improvement.

In my agency days, the most frequent complaint I received from clients concerned the poor quality of the writing our account teams produced. When I became a client, I often had the same complaint. I understand that not everyone is fortunate enough to be an excellent writer, but anyone with 16 years or more of schooling ought to be able to write grammatically correct, typo-free prose. (By the way, that ability doesn't mean you don't need an editor—I had two editors review this book.)

A generation ago, public relations would have been an odd career choice for someone who was unskilled in—let alone passionate about—writing. In fact, back then a lot of people in PR started out in journalism; one of the reasons clients hired agencies was for access to these outstanding writing skills.

When I interview candidates now, writing is always at the top of my list of essential skills even if the bulk of their writing will be in bursts of 140 characters or fewer. A person who can write clearly and succinctly has the ability to take complex subjects and talk about them in language average people can understand. Scientists talk to each other in professional shorthand that would be impenetrable to most people; a talented writer can translate.

The emphasis on strong writing has withered over the years, although its absence is hardly confined to PR. But PR is one business where excellent writing should be the table stakes to play. Many have speculated about the root causes of this widespread inability to write well. Perhaps it is not emphasized in school the way it was when I was a kid. It starts with a foundation of good grammar. My seventh-grade English teacher spent the entire year making the class memorize the parts of speech and we spent countless hours diagramming sentences. It was tedious beyond imagining, but every kid in that class knew the difference between a participle and a gerund and I bet they still do today. (I wonder if any of them are looking for some freelance work.)

# # #

I often think of a quote from one of our nation's Founding Fathers, Patrick Henry: "It is natural for man to indulge in illusions of hope. We are apt to shut our eyes against a painful truth. For my part, whatever anguish of spirit it might cause, I am willing to know the whole truth; to know the worst, and to provide for it."

Good old Patrick. He did have a way with words. Had he lived today, he undoubtedly would have recognized and condemned the widespread denial and delusion on trading floors and in boardrooms that sowed the seeds of the financial crisis. And now, even as the US economy shows signs of improvement, there are still too many people out of work, out of homes—just plain out of luck.

Not surprisingly, a crisis of trust exists among the American people. In a 2013 Edelman study called the "Trust Barometer," fewer than 20 percent of respondents believed Big Business makes ethical and moral decisions. Fewer still believed Big Business will tell them the truth. Faith in government was even lower: fewer than 15 percent said they believe the government makes ethical and moral decisions or tells the truth.

While we should remember that the vast majority of corporate directors and officers are honest, decent and repelled by the actions of a few miscreants, unfortunately all of business is sullied by these few. Even companies that were in no way connected to the Wall Street meltdown have lost the trust of some of their employees, customers and communities as they took the necessary and painful steps to survive in a deep recession: layoffs, plant closings, and restructurings.

We can't fix the past, but we can improve the future. And one of the questions professional communicators get a lot is, "How can a company rebuild the bond of trust with its key stakeholders?"

The least effective way to engender trust, of course, is to declare oneself to be trustworthy. Trust is built over time, based on what companies do, not what they say. The bond of trust is forged through a variety of interactions between a company and its stakeholders. One definition of trust looks like this:

$$\text{Trust} = \text{Competence} + \text{Commitment}$$

If people believe you are competent to accomplish a task and are committed to achieving it, they will trust you with that task. If you repeatedly demonstrate competence and commitment, an ever-deeper bond can be built.

If we learned anything from the financial crisis, it's that trust takes a long time to build, and a nanosecond to destroy. To get it back, organizations must focus not on trust per se but on competence and commitment. What might that look like? Well, one place to start is with *Fortune* magazine's most admired companies. Fortune identified nine key attributes of companies with the best reputations:

- Ability to attract and retain talented people
- Quality of management
- Social responsibility to the community and the environment
- Innovativeness
- Quality of products or services
- Wise use of corporate assets
- Financial soundness
- Long-term investment value
- Effectiveness at doing business globally

If we examine each of these attributes through the "Competence + Commitment" lens, we can begin to identify the expectations that stakeholders have of a company and how to meet them. For example, a company that demonstrates both competence and commitment to product quality would be able to point to a state-of-the-art quality assurance process and a willingness to hold itself accountable for quality metrics. A company that demonstrates competence in and commitment to innovativeness hires the best talent and invests in research and development.

And, a company that demonstrates competence in and commitment to management quality acknowledges, in true Patrick Henry style, when its performance lags behind expectations and then implements a plan for improvement.

Historically, companies focused on these attributes have fared better than companies that have not. Running a business with the interests of all stakeholders in mind and embracing an appropriate degree of transparency are the best strategies a company can adopt.

It's also important for companies to consider their influencer strategy. As noted, a company can't simply declare with any credibility that it behaves in a trustworthy manner. But a third party can. Who are the people the media turn to for opinions about your company? Is a process in place to reach out to these influencers and turn them into evangelists for your company? It takes time to build these relationships—which are built, after all, on trust. Being able to leverage your relationships with these opinion leaders when hard times come can be a major advantage. It's almost impossible after the fact.

When a company is coming out of a crisis, be it a long-term financial meltdown or an explosive industrial accident, an understandable desire exists to find the one thing—the preemptive action or bold stroke—that will make the pain go away. But a CEO doesn't restore trust by signing a letter attesting to financial results or recalibrating the audit and compensation board committees. These are by no means bad things to do, but they aren't, in and of themselves, the building blocks of a trusting relationship.

Yes, trust has been strained, perhaps broken. But for the most part, human beings are a forgiving lot. Most companies that have been embroiled at one point or another in scandal or crisis have survived—and have even, in the fullness of time, thrived.

To know the worst, and to provide for it: It turns out that Patrick Henry invented issues management. Who knew?

# # #

Having served on both sides of the fence—agency and client—I have seen how to build a partnership that lasts for years, and also how to create an environment so unpleasant both parties are thrilled to say, "Good riddance."

Note to agency leaders and teams:

Your client is not an ATM. Beginning every single conversation with, "Is there budget for this?" is not an effective growth strategy. A former agency colleague tells the story of how he used to walk the halls at one client's offices, chatting people up and listening for opportunity to knock. "I guess I was a little aggressive," he told me. "There was one guy who, whenever he saw me, always reached back as if trying to hang on to his wallet. He and I laughed the first time he did it, but by the third time, I thought it actually wasn't very funny. If he felt that way, maybe others did, too. I backed off."

This may seem obvious, but stay within your budget. If you misjudged the cost, bite the bullet and tell the client before you've spent the available money and either have to eat the over-servicing or go hat in hand to the client and hope he or she can do some budget-juggling. If the client changes the specifications of the engagement, make clear what the budget implications of those changes will be—early. Nothing cools a client's ardor than budgeting $100,000 for a project and getting a bill for $150,000.

Note to clients:

I know that there are times when it's necessary, but don't make a habit of dumping a request on your agency at 4:30 on a Friday afternoon.

Spread thanks and praise lavishly, and don't be shy about singling out an individual's excellent performance—it makes the whole team feel great.

Pay promptly; if you have an issue with an invoice, get it on the table and resolved as soon as possible. Be reasonable in your budget expectations. Ask often how much the agency is over-servicing your business. The agency's best talent will do anything to avoid working on an unprofitable account—and you want the best people, right?

Finally, if you have just joined your company as the head of PR, take the time to make a careful assessment of your agency's performance before arbitrarily putting your account up for review, just to show what kind of a "take charge" leader you are.

Note to both:

My wife, Lauren, has written and performed a terrific solo show called *The Fiery Sword of Justice*. In it she hilariously recounts how growing up in an alcoholic family equipped her with just the tools she needed to thrive in a PR agency.

She tells of a conversation she had with her boss early in her career.

"You know," he said, "there are more adult children of alcoholics in PR than in any other profession. Oh, yes. It's a well-known fact. The relationship between a client and its PR agency is completely codependent. Just like in an alcoholic family. The client is the parent and has all the power. The agency is the child, and needs the client's business to survive." This is not a healthy relationship.

Remember the PRSA's definition of PR? "Public relations is a strategic communication process that builds mutually beneficial relationships between organizations and their publics." It all hinges on building a relationship between client and agency that's good for both. It takes work, but it's worth it.

# # #

Thirty-four years is a long time to do anything, but I feel like the years have flown by. I suppose that's partly because I keep ending up where I started—literally. The one thing that Rockwell & Newell, Ketchum and PwC had in common was the corner of 41st Street and Madison Avenue. From my perch on the 20th floor at PwC's headquarters, I could peer down into the 10th floor window I used to look out of at Rockwell, and the fourth-floor window of my office at Ketchum.

I have been extremely fortunate to work at a great many interesting and varied jobs. Starting a new position is always exciting because you never fully grasp how much you have learned in a job until you start a new one. Suddenly, everything you've done and have seen done by others becomes part of your bag of tricks. On the first day, you meet a lot of people, but it's too soon to know who will be your new "work spouse" and who will be your nemesis; who will help you out when you need it and who will revel in your every misstep. But most especially, you don't know who will turn out to be a lifelong friend.

I stay in touch with one or more former colleagues from every job I've ever had. Some are among the first people I call with good news or bad; some only get holiday cards and a note. But I keep up with them all. Facebook and LinkedIn have made this easy. I treasure these friends and hope that I can always be there for them (as they have so often been for me), whether they want to celebrate something great or just need a shoulder and a Kleenex.

Acknowledgements

TO THE MANY PEOPLE—PEOPLE I have worked for and those who have worked for me—without whose support I could never have been successful, thank you. This book is for you.

To the people (I hope not many) whose expectations I have failed to meet—people I have let down, people I have hurt—I apologize.

There are many people to whom I owe a debt of gratitude. Among them, Harold Burson, Chris Komisarjevsky, Peter Hirsch, Michael Goodman and Irv Schenkler were generous in their suggestions and encouragement.

My editors, Anne Glusker and Lari Bishop, are ruthless grammarians and they slashed extra words and whole pages when they did not advance the narrative. (Thanks, I needed that!) But they never edited out the fun of the stories and for that I am grateful.

And to my talented and witty wife, Lauren Letellier, thanks to you above any other. You're the one who said, "Of course you can write a book. Just get on with it, will ya?"

So I did.

About the Author

Photo: © Lauren Letellier, PHP

CHRIS ATKINS IS AN INDEPENDENT public relations consultant with 35 years of PR agency and in-house experience.

Chris joined PwC in May, 2011 and managed all internal and external communications for the firm. With nearly nine billion in revenues and 30,000 employees, PwC (US) is the largest of the "Big Four" accounting firms. He joined PwC after five years at Standard & Poor's, where he was responsible for all communications for credit ratings and indices, such as the S&P 500. He was at the forefront of S&P's crisis response regarding the role of credit ratings in the financial meltdown. Before joining S&P, he spent 26 years at several major public relations agencies. He was Managing Director of the Global Corporate Practices at Ogilvy Public Relations and Ketchum, counseling clients such as FedEx, the New York Stock Exchange and GE. While at Ketchum, Chris founded the Ketchum Reputation Lab, which used the 20+ year data set from Fortune Magazine's "America's Most Admired Corporations" survey to develop an analytical tool to inform communications strategy.

Chris also served as Chief Operating Officer of the New York office of Burson-Marsteller, and was a Vice President in the Corporate Group at Hill & Knowlton. A frequent speaker and guest lecturer at NYU and Columbia on the topic of crisis preparedness and response, Chris was named by *PR Week* as one of the "20 crisis counselors CEOs should have in their speed-dialer."

Chris is a member of the Arthur W. Page Society, and a former trustee of the Institute for Public Relations. He is the co-author of a book on corporate reputation called Image Wars: Protecting Your Company When There's No Place to Hide (1989, John Wiley & Sons). He lives with his wife, Lauren Letellier, in Manhattan.

Connect with Chris:
By email: chrisahdw@gmail.com
Via his blog: chrisatkinsrandomprthoughts.com
On Twitter: @chrisatkinspr
On Facebook: facebook.com/chrisatkinsbook